A 90-DAY

# A
# *Woman*
## OF
## PURPOSE
## AND
## POWER

## DR. MYLES MUNROE

WHITAKER
HOUSE

## A WOMAN OF PURPOSE AND POWER:
*A 90-Day Devotional*

Munroe Global
P.O. Box N9583
Nassau, Bahamas
www.munroeglobal.com
office@mumroeglobal.com

ISBN: 978-1-64123-233-3
eBook ISBN: 978-1-64123-234-0
Printed in the United States of America
© 2019 by Munroe Group of Companies Ltd.

Whitaker House
1030 Hunt Valley Circle
New Kensington, PA 15068
www.whitakerhouse.com

Library of Congress Cataloging-in-Publication Data (Pending)

1 2 3 4 5 6 7 8 9 10 11 ⨇ 26 25 24 23 22 21 20 19

# CONTENTS

# INTRODUCTION

For thirty years, Dr. Myles Munroe studied, counseled, and guided thousands of individuals to live lives of personal fulfillment and social and spiritual well-being. The knowledge and experience he gained led him to the conclusion that the central principle of life is *purpose*.

Yet, as he described in his book *Understanding the Purpose and Power of Women*, it is extremely difficult to be a woman in the twenty-first century, even though progress has been made in promoting the respect, value, and purpose of women. He writes: "Women around the world are facing the dilemma of identity. Many women are struggling to discover who they are and where they stand today—in the family, the community, and the world. At the same time that women's personal expectations and roles are changing in some nations, many men around the world still have their own opinions about the place of women and want to impose certain standards of behavior on them. Other men are uncertain about the woman's role and function, and therefore they offer little support to women who are struggling with questions of identity.

Additionally, many societies are still very much in a place of transition regarding the status of women. Because of this shift in position and roles, many women are finding themselves in either an uneasy cooperation or an uncomfortable conflict with men.

"The question of a woman's status and the issue of equal rights for women are relevant to every culture and society on the globe. The world's confusion over the place and worth of women manifests itself in a variety of ways. In industrial nations, changing roles of women in the family and society not only have brought new vocational opportunities for women but also unforeseen personal and social issues. Even though women are working the same jobs as men, on average they earn less than men and have less opportunity for advancement. Though many women are building careers, they are also still doing the majority of the child-rearing and household chores. The pace of such a life is leaving them exhausted and disillusioned. On a personal level, confusion over male/female roles and expectations has led to misunderstandings, conflicts, and unstable relationships with the opposite sex. Women today are struggling with the delicate balance of attending to the needs of both their families and their careers, job competition with men, emotional turmoil and lost income due to divorce, single parenthood, and conflicts stemming from cultural changes in the way women and men interrelate. Some women are confused about what a woman should be and how she should conduct herself because they're not sure what a woman is supposed to be responsible for anymore."

From his study of the Scriptures, Dr. Munroe believed that women have a unique and wonderful purpose in God's plan for the world. As you progress through these ninety devotionals, you will discover *A Woman's Purpose and Power* and how you were created to live harmoniously, productively, and purposefully in relationship with others. You will understand biblical truths and principles that explain women's distinct design and relationship to men, and find practical application for implementing what you learn into your daily life.

Also featured are daily Scripture readings, with one Old Testament passage and one New Testament passage for each day. Since we find our purpose only in the mind of our Maker, it is essential to read His "Manual," as Dr. Munroe liked to call the Bible, for ourselves in order to clearly see the revelation of His purposes. We must allow God's Word to dwell richly in our hearts so that, as we meditate on and absorb Scripture, it truly becomes a part of our lives.

Whenever we study the Word of God, we should also pray and ask God for wisdom. The Holy Spirit is our teacher, and we need to ask Him to illuminate the Word and give us insight.

You can discover how to live according to God's plan, so you can become all you were created to be as a unique woman made in His image—*A Woman of Purpose and Power*. May God bless you in your relationship with Him and with those He has placed in your life as you fulfill that distinct purpose.

*— Day 1 —*

# DO YOU KNOW WHERE
# YOU'RE HEADED?

*"In their hearts humans plan their course, but the* L ORD *establishes their steps."* —Proverbs 16:9

I was driving along an undeveloped street near my home one day when I saw a large sign with a beautifully painted picture of a building. The sign said, C OMING S OON. I sensed the Holy Spirit saying to me, "Did you see that?" I asked, "See what?" He said, "Did you see the finish?" I came back around to take another look at the painting, and the Holy Spirit continued, "If you were to see the men working on that project, digging up all the mud and muck, making big holes, and if you were to ask them what they were doing, they would say, 'We are building that.' They could tell you exactly where they were headed." I have never forgotten that lesson.

I have a question for you: Is your life similar to that? If someone were to ask you where you're going, could you answer that you're headed somewhere? Could you specify where? Are you so clear about your dream that you could paint a picture of it?

If you know where you're going, then when someone doesn't understand the reason for "the mud, the muck, the water, and the hole," it doesn't matter. Everything might look in disarray, but you know it is part of the process. And when you're in the midst of the process, your life might not seem like it's becoming anything. But take careful note: there's a painting of you. God has painted it for you in His Word. Anytime you get bogged down, every time you get discouraged, you can look at that painting.

We may be able to see the outcome of God's purposes for our lives twenty years into the future—or only one day ahead. Yet if we are living in God's plans for us, we have found the key to our existence.

Dear Father,

You are the Creator, the Maker of all things—including me. You have a purpose for my creation beyond anything I can easily understand. Help me to keep my eyes upon You and Your Word as You reveal my purpose on this earth. In Jesus's name, amen.

⌒

*Thought*: If someone were to ask you where you're going in life, what would you answer?

*Readings*: Proverbs 16:1–20; Matthew 6:1–16

# SEEKING IDENTITY

*"We have not received the spirit of the world but the Spirit who is from God, that we may understand what God has freely given us."* —1 Corinthians 2:12

There is a tremendous pull by our culture for women to seek identity in all the wrong places. A woman's true identity is not in her intelligence, her appearance, her wealth, her job, others' opinions, or even her husband and children.

If you don't understand yourself, you don't yet possess yourself. That is why people who don't know who they are imitate other people and become someone other than who they were created to be. If you don't know what you were born to be and do, then you become a victim of other people's opinions. Understanding who made you and who you are is crucial so that others do not take possession of your life. When you have understanding, you know what to do with your life.

A woman first needs to find her identity in who she is in Christ—God's beloved child. It is only as she does this that she can be fulfilled and carry out His plans for her. Regardless of what culture and society may say to the contrary, the highest worth and dignity were given to women by God in creation. When a woman submits to God, Christ will work in her and through her by His Spirit. In this way, she will be enabled to accomplish all the purposes He has for her—but in His strength, not her own.

You may be missing out in regard to fulfilling the specific purposes for which you were created. God is saying to you, "I want you to stop trying to be like someone else and be who you are."

The apostle Paul said, *"Follow my example, as I follow the example of Christ"* (1 Corinthians 11:1). In other words, "When I look like Christ, imitate me." The only thing we are to imitate of what we see in other people is the life of Christ.

God has special plans for you, if you will seek to become who He created you to be. He has given you your personality and gifts for a specific reason. *"For we are God's handiwork created in Christ Jesus to do good works, which God prepared in advance for us to do"* (Ephesians 2:10).

God made you unique because of the purpose He had in mind for you.

*Thought*: God made you unique because of the purpose He had in mind for you.

*Readings*: Psalm 139:13–18; Galatians 2:20

# UNDERSTANDING YOUR PURPOSE

*"Take my yoke upon you and learn from me, for I am gentle and humble in heart, and you will find rest for your souls."*
—Matthew 11:29

The great challenge of life is understanding life. When life throws us a curveball, we often just play games and fake it. Many times, we have to guess and then wonder endlessly if our guesses will work.

What we lack is understanding. David, the great king of Israel, made an observation regarding this very issue. By divine inspiration, he spoke of the moral and social chaos in his community and described the root cause of humanity's confusion, frustration, and self-destruction: "[They] *know nothing, they understand nothing. They walk about in darkness; all the foundations of the earth are shaken"* (Psalm 82:5).

This text declares that the reason why the people of the earth are so confused and filled with problems is not because there are no answers but because we don't understand our Creator. We don't know His principles, His purpose, His nature, or His precepts.

The greatest enemy of mankind is *ignorance of self.* Nothing is more frustrating than not knowing who you are or what to do with what you have. All of humanity's problems are a result of this major dilemma. Essentially, the dilemma is that we lack understanding. Without understanding, life is an experiment, and frustration is the reward.

But learning God's ways will transform your spirit, your mind, and your outlook. When you present yourself to God and learn from Him, you will begin to understand His purpose. *"The law of the* LORD *is perfect, refreshing the soul. The statutes of the* LORD *are trustworthy, making wise the simple"* (Psalm 19:7).

The greatest way for you to find purpose is to yield your life to the Manufacturer. You shouldn't come to God because it's the religious thing to do. You shouldn't come to God because "everybody" is doing it. You shouldn't come to God because it's good to be a part of the church. You should come to God because you want to find out how not to waste your life. No one knows you like the One who made you. That's the bottom line.

We are so special to God that He sent His only Son to die for us. There must be something unique about each one of us for God to want us to receive salvation so that we can fulfill the purpose for which He gave us life. We need to seek Him earnestly in order to discover that purpose. *"You will seek me and find me when you seek me with all your heart"* (Jeremiah 29:13).

⁓

*Thought:* The greatest way for you to find purpose is to yield your life to the Manufacturer.

*Readings:* Psalm 19; Matthew 11:25–28

# SEVEN PRINCIPLES OF PURPOSE

"[God] *works out everything in conformity with the purpose of his will.*"                              —Ephesians 1:11

The source of so many of our problems in this world, including the misunderstanding and mistreatment of women, is that we have lost our understanding of what it means to be human as God created us. We have lost our sense of purpose. I am convinced that, in every country in the world, both women and men are suffering from this ignorance of purpose. The best thing for us to do is to discover and live in the original plan of the One who created humanity. Only then will we learn the inherent nature and rights of women and men, so that both female and male can live in freedom and fulfillment.

The following seven principles of purpose will help us to understand God's original intent for us in creation.

1.  God is a God of purpose.
2.  God created everything with a purpose.
3.  Not every purpose is known to us because we have lost our understanding of God's original intent for us.
4.  Where purpose is not known, abuse is inevitable.
5.  To discover the purpose of something, never ask the creation; ask the creator.
6.  We find our purpose only in the mind of our Maker.
7.  God's purpose is the key to our fulfillment.

God is a purposeful Being. He purposes, He plans, and then He carries out His plans. God always knew what He wanted to create before He made it; similarly, He always knows what He wants to carry out before He accomplishes it.

This theme is found throughout the Bible, which we can consider God's handbook, or manual, for our lives. Here are various expressions of His purposeful nature:

*And God said, "Let there be light," and there was light.*
(Genesis 1:3)

*The plans of the LORD stand firm forever, the purposes of his heart through all generations.*          (Psalm 33:11)

*The LORD Almighty has sworn, "Surely, as I have planned, so it will be, and as I have purposed, so it will happen."*
(Isaiah 14:24)

*As the rain and the snow come down from heaven, and do not return to it without watering the earth and making it bud and flourish, so that it yields seed for the sower and bread for the eater, so is my word that goes out from my mouth: It will not return to me empty, but will accomplish what I desire and achieve the purpose for which I sent it.*     (Isaiah 55:10–11)

*God…has saved us and called us to a holy life—not because of anything we have done but because of his own purpose and grace. This grace was given us in Christ Jesus before the beginning of time.*          (2 Timothy 1:8–9)

We have been created purposefully by God. Only when we fully understand this concept will we see how important it is for our well-being that we discover God's intent for us.

⌒

*Thought*: God is a God of purpose.

*Readings*: Meditate on the above passages from the Old and New Testaments.

# GOD WILL FULFILL HIS PURPOSES

*"The plans of the LORD stand firm forever, the purposes of his heart through all generations."* —Psalm 33:11

God is purposeful, and He always carries out His purposes. Let's review some Scripture verses from Isaiah and Hebrews that illustrate a vital aspect of God's purposeful nature.

> The LORD Almighty has sworn, "Surely, as I have planned, so it will be, and as I have purposed, so it will happen."
> (Isaiah 14:24)

The first part of this verse states that God has sworn an oath. Now, when people swear an oath, they have to find something higher than themselves by which to swear. As we read in Hebrews 6:16, *"People swear by someone greater than themselves, and the oath confirms what is said and puts an end to all argument."* We usually swear by the Bible or by some great institution. But when God swears an oath, there is no one above Him. So, He has to swear by Himself.

If you were called to be a witness in court, you would be asked to swear on the Bible, "I swear to tell the truth, the whole truth, and nothing but the truth, so help me, God." If you were to lie, it would be the same as desecrating the integrity of the Bible, and you would destroy your own integrity as well.

When God swears an oath regarding something, He fulfills what He has sworn to do, because He is totally faithful to Himself. God doesn't want us to have any doubt about this aspect of His nature.

*Because God wanted to make the unchanging nature of his purpose very clear to the heirs of what was promised, he confirmed it with an oath.* (Hebrews 6:17)

We can be assured that God will fulfill His purposes for us as we allow Christ the Redeemer to restore us to Him and to the purposes He has for us.

⌒

*Thought*: God is purposeful and He always carries out His purposes.

*Readings:* Psalm 33; Hebrews 6:13–20

# GOD CREATED EVERYTHING
# WITH A PURPOSE

*"Star differs from star in splendor ["glory" NKJV]."*
—1 Corinthians 15:41

Purpose is the original intent of a creator in the creation of something. It is what is in the creator's mind that causes him to fashion his product in a certain manner. In short, purpose motivates the action of creation. This results in precision production.

Everything that God has made in this life has a purpose. One of the essential principles of purpose is that "the purpose of something determines its nature or design." We can fight against God's purposes for us, but if we do, we will be unfulfilled and frustrated. He made us the way we are for His purposes and for our benefit.

Since God is a God of purpose, He never created anything hoping that it would turn out to be something viable. He first decided what it was to be, then He made it. He always begins with a finished product in mind.

Consider these questions:

+ Why are humans different from animals?
+ Why is a bird different from a fish?
+ Why is the sun different from the moon?
+ Why does one star differ from another star?
+ Why are women different from men?

I will answer these questions with this statement: Everything is the way it is because of why it was created, because of its purpose. The *why* dictates the design. God created everything with the ability to fulfill its purpose. Therefore, to understand how we function as human beings, we have to go to the Manual given to us by the Designer and Manufacturer who created us.

*"People have one kind of flesh, animals have another, birds another and fish another"* (1 Corinthians 15:39). Of course, the word *"flesh"* in this instance does not refer to meat; instead, it refers to the nature of the creature—its characteristic design. God determined that human beings would be different from animals in their nature. He also determined that birds and fish would have distinct natures. The passage goes on to say,

> *There are also heavenly bodies and there are earthly bodies; but the splendor* ["glory" NKJV] *of the heavenly bodies is one kind, and the splendor* ["glory" NKJV] *of the earthly bodies is another. The sun has one kind of splendor* ["glory" NKJV], *the moon another and the stars another; and star differs from star in splendor* ["glory" NKJV].     (1 Corinthians 15:40–41)

The sun is meant to do a job that the moon isn't supposed to do, so God created the moon different from the sun. The moon is made to do its job, and no other job. The moon does not give light; it reflects light. Therefore, God did not put any light on the moon. God also made stars of different sizes and luminosity, for His own purposes. The point is that God made everything the way it is because of what it is supposed to do. And that includes us!

⌒

*Thought*: To understand how we function as human beings, we have to go to the Manual given to us by the Designer and Manufacturer who created us.

*Readings*: Genesis 1:1–26; Ephesians 1:3–14

# NOT EVERY PURPOSE IS KNOWN TO US

*"Your word is a lamp for my feet, a light on my path."*
—Psalm 119:105

Everything God created has a purpose and is designed according to that purpose. However, not every purpose is known to us. Humanity has lost its knowledge of God's purposes. It has not respected the fact that God's creation and His directions for living were established for a specific reason and that, if this purpose is abandoned, we will never function properly as human beings. The result of this abandonment has been debilitating for us: we have grown further and further away from God's original intent and design, so that we function less and less as we were meant to. This has left us incomplete, frustrated, and in conflict with one another.

The first chapter of Romans explains that when people reject or are ignorant of the purposes of God, they end up continually abusing themselves. They abuse their bodies, their minds, their relationships, and their talents.

> *Although they knew God, they neither glorified him as God nor gave thanks to him, but their thinking became futile and their foolish hearts were darkened.* (Romans 1:21)

This verse describes those who did not know the purpose of God and did not even care to find out what it is. Even though they knew something about God and His ways, they did not want Him in their lives. They did not want to know what He wanted them to know. They were saying, in effect, "Keep Your opinions about who we are to Yourself, God. We know You made us, but mind Your own business. We know You're there, but leave us alone."

The next verses tell us the result of their decision: *"Although they claimed to be wise, they became fools"* (Romans 1:22). They *"exchanged the truth about God for a lie"* and *"exchanged natural sexual relations for unnatural ones"* (verse 25–26).

When does the exchange of natural for unnatural take place? It takes place when purpose is either ignored or unknown. *"Furthermore, just as they did not think it worthwhile to retain the knowledge of God, so God gave them over to a depraved mind, so that they do what ought not to be done"* (verse 28). They didn't think it worthwhile to find out God's purpose for the world or to retain the knowledge of God as to why He made humanity. They didn't check to find out why God made women and men. They didn't try to find out what God knows about the things He has made. They didn't want to know, so they relied on their own inclinations.

The above statements from Romans are a description of humanity as a whole. We have rejected knowing God and His purposes, and so God's original intent for us has not been communicated in many of our cultures and traditions. It has been lost or obscured. Instead, distorted views have been passed down, so that people do not know how to relate to one another as they were meant to. This is the situation people often find themselves in, and why it is essential for us to recover our original purpose in God.

⌒

*Thought*: We have grown further and further away from God's original intent and design, so that we function less and less as we were meant to.

*Readings*: Psalm 119:97–112; Romans 1:16–32

# WHERE PURPOSE IS UNKNOWN, ABUSE IS INEVITABLE

*"There is a way that appears to be right, but in the end it leads to death."* —Proverbs 14:12

You cannot move away from God and be truly successful. You cannot cut off your relationship with the Manufacturer and expect to find genuine parts somewhere else. When you ignore the warranty, any part you try to find on your own will not be genuine. You cannot develop into a better "product" without the help of the Manufacturer.

If we think we can find out how to be a better person without God, we are in trouble, for the consequences are serious. When we believe that we don't need God, we get worse and worse. How many people have been suffering from these very consequences?

*"Many are the plans in a person's heart, but it is the* LORD's *purpose that prevails"* (Proverbs 19:21). We have many plans, but God has a purpose. Our plans may not be in harmony with God's purpose. I think it is appropriate to include the concept of opinions or perceptions in the word *"plans."* We have many opinions and perceptions regarding what things should be like or what they are for, but God has a purpose for everything that He made. Therefore, what you think the purpose of something is, and what its purpose actually is, could be different.

The problem is that, if your plans are not in keeping with God's purpose, then you will either suffer yourself or inflict abuse on others, because where purpose is not known, abuse is inevitable. If you don't know the purpose of something, all you will do is abuse it, no matter how sincere, committed, serious, or innocent you are.

If you don't want to live in God's purpose for mankind, then you will end up doing yourself harm in some way. God has created us with gifts and talents that are intended to be used to fulfill His purposes. Yet since we often don't know how they are to be used, we take the talents He has given us and use them against ourselves and others.

Remember that God did not venture out into the manufacturing business hoping He could create something that would work. He started out with an original design in mind, and His finished product parallels His intended purpose. He is the only One who knows how humanity is intended to successfully function.

~

*Thought*: God has created us with gifts and talents that are intended to be used to fulfill His purposes.

*Readings*: Proverbs 14:1–2; Ephesians 5:1–20

# TO DISCOVER PURPOSE, NEVER ASK THE CREATION—ASK THE CREATOR

*"Yet you, LORD, are our Father. We are the clay, you are the potter; we are all the work of your hand."*  —Isaiah 64:8

We have seen that nobody knows a product and how it should work better than the one who made it. In the same way, the one who created the product is the best one to fix it when it has become marred. When a potter works on a pot and sees that it has a flaw in it, the potter either remolds the clay and starts over, or if the pot already has been fired in an oven, the potter has to smash it and start over.

Now, when the clay starts talking back to the potter, something is wrong. (See Isaiah 29:16.) The potter knows better than the pot how the pot should be fashioned. The pot can't say to the potter, "You shouldn't have made me this way," because the pot can't see the whole picture, the way the potter can. When it comes to the relationship between males and females and society's devaluation of women, we have too often murmured against the Potter rather than trying to understand how and why we were created. Moreover, our substitutes for His master design are flawed. Some of us need to have our attitudes, perspectives, and lives remolded. A few of us have gone so far in the wrong direction that we may need a total overhaul. God's principles are very serious and very awesome, but also very necessary for the restoration of humanity to God's purposes.

So if you want to discover the purpose of something, never ask the creation; ask the one who made it. The creation might not think it has any worth, but the creator knows what it is made of.

Many people do not think they have any worth or purpose. Yet the first chapter of our Manual tells us, *"God saw all that he had made, and it was very good"* (Genesis 1:31). There is something good in God's creation, no matter how confused it looks to us. There is something good about every person, even though it may be hard to find. There is something good about everything God has made. We need to go to Him to find the good purposes for which He has made us. *"For it is God who works in you to will and to act in order to fulfill his good purpose"* (Philippians 2:13).

*Thought*: The one who created the product is the best one to fix it when it has become marred.

*Readings*: Jeremiah 18:1–6; Philippians 2:12–16

# — *Day 10* —
## WE FIND OUR PURPOSE ONLY
## IN OUR MAKER

*"As for God, his way is perfect: the LORD's word is flawless; he shields all who take refuge in him."* —Psalm 18:30

When we try to mend our relationships or change society using our own methods, we never totally succeed, and we often utterly fail. We fail because we are trying to bring about change for the wrong reasons and using the wrong methods. That is why we need to go back to the Manufacturer and receive His instructions for our lives. The only way for us to succeed is to discover and live in the purposes of our Maker, by undergoing a transformation in the way we think about ourselves as human beings.

Romans 12:1–2 encourages us to give ourselves to God so that we may receive His principles for living rather than conforming to this world's pattern of living:

> *Offer your bodies as a living sacrifice, holy and pleasing to God—this is your true and proper worship. Do not conform to the pattern of this world, but be transformed by the renewing of your mind. Then you will be able to test and approve what God's will is—his good, pleasing and perfect will.*

In other words, we are not to conform to this world's opinions of humanity's purpose but be transformed into God's original intent in creation, so that we can live in peace with ourselves and others. We do this by presenting our bodies to God, so they can line up with His purpose for our bodies, and by presenting our minds to Him, so they can line up with His purpose for our minds. Our minds are to be transformed as they are renewed.

Then, we will truly be able to know *what God's will is—his good, pleasing and perfect will.*"

Many of us don't know God's perfect purpose for our bodies. We've been abusing them—selling them cheaply, filling them with alcohol, drugs, nicotine, or too much food. We've been making a mess of our lives.

Our bodies are meant to be God's temple. When you present your body to the Manufacturer, what does He do with it? He fills it with His own Spirit, so you can be filled with His life and purpose. *"Do you not know that your bodies are temples of the Holy Spirit, who is in you, whom you have received from God? You are not your own"* (1 Corinthians 6:19).

When you present your spirit to the Manufacturer, it becomes *"the candle of the LORD"* (Proverbs 20:27 KJV), an expression of the light of God. It is the same way when you present your mind and soul to your Maker. They are renewed by His Word, which is a light for your path. (See Psalm 119:105.) David said, *"The law of the LORD is perfect, converting the soul; the testimony of the LORD is sure, making wise the simple"* (Psalm 19:7 NKJV). God's ways will transform your spirit, your mind, and your outlook. When you present yourself to God and learn from Him, you will understand His purpose.

Therefore, in order to pursue God's purpose, you first must present yourself to God, so that you can *know* His perfect will. Then you will be transformed, so that you can *do* His perfect will. In this way, His good purposes will be fulfilled in you.

⌒

*Thought:* We need to undergo a transformation in the way we think about ourselves as human beings.

*Readings:* Psalm 18:1–2, 30–36; Romans 12

# GOD'S PURPOSE IS THE KEY TO OUR FULFILLMENT

*"Forgetting what is behind and straining toward what is ahead, I press on toward the goal to win the prize for which God has called me heavenward in Christ Jesus."*
—Philippians 3:13–14

Since everything God created was intentional, we can conclude that the female, as well as the male, was created intentionally. God didn't wonder why He made the woman or what her purpose should be after He created her. He was very clear about why He made this wonderful creation, and therefore we don't have to guess about her. The female was created to help fulfill God's eternal purpose. His eternal purpose is great, and within His larger purpose, He has many smaller purposes. Both the female and the male are to discover their individual purposes, which are part of God's larger plan.

The key thoughts we have been addressing in this devotional are that God has a purpose for everything, and that He will always accomplish His purpose in the end. The best way to experience fulfillment in your life is to find God's purpose and then work with Him to fulfill it. In the previous devotional, we read, *"Therefore, I urge you, brothers and sisters, in view of God's mercy, to offer your bodies as a living sacrifice, holy and pleasing to God—this is your true and proper worship"* (Romans 12:1). Becoming what He has purposed for us is an act of worship to our Creator.

In the devotionals that follow, we will learn more about the purpose, nature, and design of the woman as she was created in the image of God and as she relates to the man. These are God's ideal purposes for women and men, which we desire to move toward. However, we must keep in mind that entering into God's purposes will be a continual process of learning and transformation. Therefore, we need to be patient with ourselves. We are starting where we are now—not at the place we should be, and not at the place at which we will arrive.

In regard to our spiritual growth, Paul taught us that we are to forget the things that are behind us and reach for what is ahead of us. We are to press on to the mark, which is the *"high calling of God in Christ Jesus"* (Philippians 3:14 KJV). When Jesus came to earth, He showed us the mark that we are to hit. So whatever He says is what we're supposed to pursue. He showed us God's original plan so that we could have something to aim at. We should never accept what we currently have as the norm. Even though it may be the current trend, if it's not what God intended, it's abnormal. We should never live so below our privilege that we begin to believe a lie and call it truth.

When we—both women and men—gain an understanding of our uniqueness and purpose in God, we will be able to assist one another in properly understanding and fulfilling the lives God created us to live. We will then also be able to live in right relationship with God, and in the freedom and blessings He planned for us in creation. What's more, when we mend the broken relationships between female and male, both of whom are created in the image of God, we will begin to see healing and new purpose for the individuals, communities, and nations of our world.

⟳

*Thought*: Becoming what God has purposed for us is an act of worship to our Creator.

*Readings*: Psalm 95:1–7; Philippians 3:7–16

# GOOD VERSUS BEST

*"'I have the right to do anything,' you say—but not everything is beneficial. 'I have the right to do anything'—but not everything is constructive."* —1 Corinthians 10:23

Wouldn't it be sad to be serious and committed and faithful—to the wrong thing? It would be terrible to be busy doing the wrong things your entire life. It is possible to do good things but not the things that are best based on God's purposes for you.

There are many good people who are pursuing relationships, careers, and goals in life that are not best for them. What we have to concern ourselves with is living effectively.

God created each of us with a purpose that is right for us. Suppose Jesus had become a priest in the Sanhedrin, the highest council and tribunal of the Jews. That would have been a good thing. Suppose He had become a member of the Pharisees and been one of the leaders in the social structure of Galilee and Judea. That would have been a good thing. Suppose He had become a social worker, helping the poor, feeding multitudes of people every day with bread and fish. Would that have been a good thing? Of course. Suppose He had devoted every hour to healing the sick and raising the dead. That would have been a good thing, wouldn't it? Yet none of these things would have been the right thing for Him in fulfilling His chief purpose of being the Savior of humanity.

Jesus was always able to say, in effect, "I know the purpose for My life. Don't distract Me with things that are merely good. I must pursue the highest purpose."

Discovering our purpose enables us to stop wasting our lives and start fulfilling our potential. We must be careful not to become sidetracked along the way. The greatest way to destroy someone is to distract that person from his or her true purpose.

In the Old Testament, Nehemiah fulfilled an important purpose in life, but he might have been sidetracked. He was a Hebrew in exile serving as cupbearer to the king of Persia when he heard that Jerusalem was in a broken-down condition. He was distressed over this, and he determined, "I've got to repair the city." So he prayed, and he obtained permission from the king to rebuild the wall of Jerusalem. God's favor was on his plans because this was the purpose for which he had been created. He went and started to rebuild the wall with the help of the remnant of Jews in Jerusalem.

Some men near Jerusalem didn't like what Nehemiah was doing, and they tried to stop him. Yet Nehemiah told them, *"I am carrying on a great project and cannot go down. Why should the work stop while I leave it and go down to you?"* (Nehemiah 6:3). In the same way, don't allow yourself to be distracted from your primary purpose in God!

*Thought*: Discovering our purpose enables us to stop wasting our lives and start fulfilling our potential.

*Readings*: Nehemiah 6:1–15; Galatians 6:7–9

# THE GOLD INSIDE YOU

*"I praise you because I am fearfully and wonderfully made;*
*your works are wonderful, I know that full well."*
— Psalm 139:14

In the mid-twentieth century, in Bangkok, Thailand, the government wanted to build a large highway through a village. In the path of the planned road was a Buddhist monastery with a little chapel, so they had to relocate the monastery—including a heavy, eleven-foot clay statue of Buddha—to another place. When the workers transported the statue of Buddha to the new location and began to lower it into place, unexpectedly, the clay on the statue started to crumble and fall off. The people were afraid because this was a precious religious symbol to them, and they didn't want it to be destroyed. Suddenly, the workers stared in amazement because, as the clay fell away, they saw that the statue was pure gold underneath! Before the statue was moved, people thought it was worth about fifty thousand dollars. Today, that golden Buddha is worth millions and, because of the story behind it, is visited by hundreds of thousands of people every year.

This story illustrates that what we can see is not necessarily what really is. I believe that many of us are living as clay vessels when, in reality, we are pure gold inside. This gold is the dreams we have—or once had—for our lives that are not yet reality, the God-given gifts and talents that we have not yet developed, the purpose for our lives that is not yet fulfilled. How do you remove the clay and uncover the gold within you? Your dreams, talents, and desires can be refined in a process of discovering and fulfilling your life's vision so that the pure gold of your unique and personal gifts to this world can truly shine forth.

> Father, You have created me with unique and precious gifts, like gold. Help me to discover these gifts and use them to bless the world around me. In Jesus's name, amen.

*Thought*: Many of us are living as clay vessels when we are pure gold inside.

*Readings*: Psalm 139:1–16; 1 Peter 2:9–10

# DON'T GIVE UP ON A
# PURPOSEFUL LIFE

*"I will repay ["restore to" NKJV] you for the years the locusts have eaten."* —Joel 2:25

Are you still questioning what your life is about? I know it's not easy to take a hard look at yourself, but it's necessary if you're going to discover your true purpose in life. You will be busy doing meaningful work when you learn why you are here. Even at twelve years of age, Jesus was busy with His purpose. (See Luke 2:41–49.) Isn't that an exciting way to live? Don't give up on having a purposeful life, no matter what your age. Get busy with the right thing.

I don't have a "job" anymore, but I used to. I worked for the Bahamas government for twelve years. I taught junior high school for five years. I worked in a food store before that, packing shelves. I worked in a warehouse lifting boxes. I worked in an ad firm, doing advertisements, drawings, and so forth. These were learning experiences. Then I found my true work of helping others understand how to manifest their God-given leadership potential. I don't wake up in the morning and "go" to work. I wake up and become what God created me to be.

Jesus said, *"Let your light so shine before men, that they may see your good works, and glorify your Father which is in heaven"* (Matthew 5:16 KJV). When other people see your work, when they see you manifesting what God put into you, they will glorify God. You were born to do something so awesome that only God could get the credit for it.

God desires that all people find their purpose and fulfill it. I once spoke about purpose at a church in Baton Rouge, Louisiana.

A woman came up to me after the service and said, "I'm fifty-six years old, brother. Where were you fifty-six years ago?" I asked, "What do you mean?" She replied, "You're the first person ever to come into my life and help me understand that I have a reason for living—and I can't give an account for fifty-six years right now."

Sometimes, people begin to feel the way that woman did; they're distressed because they've wasted so much time. If this is your situation, don't be discouraged. One of the wonderful things about God is that He has a way of restoring the years that the locusts have eaten. (See Joel 2:23–26.) When you go to Him, He knows how to make up for the time that you've lost.

Yet God would prefer that we follow Him and know our purpose all our lives. That is why the Word of God says very strongly to young people, *"Remember your Creator in the days of your youth"* (Ecclesiastes 12:1). God wants you to remember the Manufacturer early so that He can set you on course for your entire life.

We have only one life, and we have to make that life count if we are ever to fulfill our purpose. Remember, a God-given purpose can be accomplished only through His guidance and strength. *"Now to him who is able to do immeasurably more than all we ask or imagine, according to his power that is at work within us"* (Ephesians 3:20).

⌒

*Thought:* You were born to do something so awesome that only God could get the credit for it.

*Readings:* Psalm 27:7–14; Ephesians 3:14–21

— *Day 15* —

# PURPOSE DIRECTS YOUR
# PRAYER LIFE

*"Your kingdom come, your will be done, on earth as it is in heaven."* —Matthew 6:10

Praying does not mean convincing God to do your will, but doing His will through your will. Therefore, the key to effective prayer is understanding God's purpose for your life, the reason you exist—as a human being in general and as an individual specifically. This is an especially important truth to remember: once you understand your purpose, it becomes the "raw material," the foundational matter, for your prayer life. God's will is the authority of your prayers. Prayer calls forth what God has already purposed and predestined—continuing His work of creation and carrying out His plans for the earth.

> *In him we were also chosen, having been predestined according to the plan of him who works out everything in conformity with the purpose of his will.* (Ephesians 1:11)

The Father works out everything *"in conformity with the purpose of his will."* In this way, your purpose in God is the foundational material for your prayers regarding provision, healing, deliverance, power, protection, endurance, patience, authority, faith, praise, thanksgiving, confidence, assurance, boldness, and peace, for the supply of all your needs.

Some people say they do not know what to pray for. The answer is that we are not to ask God for anything outside of our purpose. *"When you ask, you do not receive, because you ask with wrong motives, that you may spend what you get on your pleasures"*

(James 4:3). If we ask for what is contrary to our purpose, we will be frustrated. Jesus always prayed for God's will to be done, then worked to accomplish it.

Everything you need is available to fulfill your purpose. All that God is, and all that He has, may be received through prayer. The measure of our appropriation of God's grace is determined by the measure of our prayers.

Father, I do not want to accomplish my will, but Your will. Lead me to conform my prayers and myself to the purpose of Your will. In Jesus's name, amen.

*Thought*: Purpose is the raw material for your prayer life.

*Readings*: Daniel 2; 2 Thessalonians 1:11–12

# CREATED IN HIS IMAGE

*"So God created man in his own image, in the image of God*
*he created him; male and female he created them."*
—Genesis 1:27 (NIV84)

To be a woman of purpose and power, it's essential to understand the foundations of God's purposes for both women and men on earth. Mankind was made in the image of God. When God made humanity, He essentially drew man out of Himself, so that the essence of man would be just like Him. Since *"God is spirit"* (John 4:24), He created man as spirit. Spirit is eternal. Mankind was created as an eternal being, because God is eternal.

It is important to recognize that we are not yet talking about male and female. It was *mankind* that God created in His image. Again, man is spirit, and spirits have no gender. The Bible never talks about a male or female spirit.

What was the reason God created mankind in His image? He didn't create any of the animals or plants in His image. He didn't even make angels in His image. Man is the only being of God's creation that is like Him.

God created mankind for relationship with Himself—to be His family, His offspring, spiritual children of God. It is the nature of God to love and to give. He wanted a being who could be the object of His love and grace. He wanted man to be the recipient of all that He is and all that He has.

The fact that mankind was created in God's image is an awesome revelation about our relationship to Him. God desired children who would be like Himself. Yet He didn't just desire it and then walk away without doing anything about it. He conceived His desire and made it a reality.

In the New Testament, Jesus both affirmed and exemplified God's love for us. He said, *"For God so loved the world that He gave His only begotten Son"* (John 3:16 NKJV). *"He gave."* He gave because He loved. You cannot love without giving. When you love, you give. It's automatic. Yet in order to give love in a way that is truly fulfilling, the receiver has to be like the giver in nature; otherwise, the love would not be complete. You cannot give in a meaningful way to something that is not like you, because it cannot receive your gift in a way that will satisfy your giving. Giving is only complete when the receiver and the giver are alike. God desired a shared and mutual love, not a one-sided love.

~

*Thought*: When God made man, He essentially drew man out of Himself, so that the essence of man would be just like Him.

*Readings*: Genesis 1:26–28; Acts 17:24–28

41

# CREATED FOR LOVE

*"We love because [God] first loved us."*　　—1 John 4:19

W e continue to explore the theme of how God created man as spirit so that He and man could share fellowship. The ultimate purpose behind the creation of "man"—both male and female— was love. The Scripture tells us that *"God is love"* (1 John 4:8, 16). What I especially like about this statement is that God doesn't just give love, He doesn't just show love—He *is* love. He desires to share His love with us because love is His essential quality.

God has many other qualities besides love that we could list. He is righteous, holy, omnipotent, and almighty. He is all of these wonderful things and so many more. God could be all of these other attributes and still exist by Himself in isolation. However, it is the nature of love to give of itself, and it cannot give in isolation. In order for love to be fulfilled, it has to have someone to love, and it has to give to its beloved.

*"I am the LORD, and there is no other; apart from me there is no God"* (Isaiah 45:5). There is no other God besides the Lord, yet He is a God of relationship, not isolation. He desires someone of His nature and likeness whom He can love. Therefore, God's primary motivation in the creation of humanity was love. He created men and women because He wanted to share His love with beings like Himself, beings created in His image. This truth is amazing to me!

God looked at what He had created, and here were these beautiful duplicates of Himself to fulfill His love. This is not an abstract concept. This means that the entire human race—including you and me—was created by God to be loved by Him.

We must remember that the only reason we can have this fellowship with God is that He made mankind to be spirit, just as He is Spirit. That is why Jesus tells us that *"God is spirit, and his worshipers must worship in the Spirit and in truth"* (John 4:24).

Although God is our Creator, He has always emphasized that He is also our Father. It wasn't His desire to be primarily thought of by us as an awesome God or a *"consuming fire"* (Deuteronomy 4:24). Although, at times, it is difficult for our religious minds to grasp this concept, God wants us to approach Him as a child would a loving father. *"Let us then approach the throne of grace with confidence, so that we may receive mercy and find grace to help us in our time of need"* (Hebrews 4:16).

God created human beings so that He could have someone to love, someone who would walk with Him and work with Him in His purposes for the earth. That is why, no matter how many relationships you have or how many gifts you buy for others, in the end, you aren't going to be satisfied until you love God. God must have the primary place in your life. Your love was designed to be fulfilled in Him.

~

*Thought*: God desires to share His love with us because love is His essential quality.

*Readings*: Psalm 103; 1 John 4:7–21

# TWO PHYSICAL HOUSES

*"So God created man in his own image, in the image of God he created him; male and female he created them."*
—Genesis 1:27 (NIV84)

In creation, God placed mankind in two physical houses: male and female. This means that "man"—the spirit—exists within every male and every female. The essence of both male and female is the resident spirit within them, called "man." This fact is often overlooked, so I want to repeat it: according to the Bible, all people—males and females alike—are man. Genesis 5:1–2 says, *"When God created man, he made him in the likeness of God. He created them male and female and blessed them. And when they were created, he called them [together] 'man'"* (NIV84).

Why did God take man, who is spirit, and put him in two separate physical entities rather than just one? It was because He wanted man to fulfill two distinct purposes. We'll explore the significance of this fact in later devotionals. For now, we need to remember that the spirit-man has no gender and that, in order to fulfill His eternal purposes, God used two physical forms to express the spiritual being made in His image.

In the Bible, when God speaks to humanity, He uses the term *man*. He doesn't address the male or the female unless He's talking to individuals. Instead, He talks to the man within them both. He addresses the spirit-man. God deals with our inner being. (See Ephesians 3:16.) Many of us are preoccupied by the outward manifestation of male or female, when we should be focusing first on the spirit-man. Paul said in Galatians 3:28 that in the body of Christ there is neither male nor female, neither slave nor master.

Thus, the person who lives inside you—the essential you—is the spirit-man. Although males and females have differences, they are of the same essence. Since human beings fellowship with God and worship Him through their spirits, this means that men and women both have direct spiritual access to God and are individually responsible to Him.

*Thought*: God used two physical forms to express the spiritual being made in His image.

*Readings*: Genesis 5:1–2; Galatians 3:26–29

# GOD'S GOOD IDEA

*"I have loved you with an everlasting love; I have drawn
you with unfailing kindness."* —Jeremiah 31:3

God did not create the woman as an afterthought but as an integral part of His plan in creation. As such, He designed and built her in His love and with particular care. Her uniqueness is a reflection of God's purposes and design for her.

Women, you don't understand how special you are! Adam hadn't even imagined the woman, but God had her particularly in mind. In Genesis 2:18, God said, *"It is not good for the man to be alone. I will make a helper suitable for him."* In essence, Adam was fumbling around in the bush thinking up animals' names (see verses 19–20), and God said, "This is not good. This man needs help." So it was God who said that the man needed the woman. You are God's idea and His unique creation.

Women, no matter what any man might say about you, no matter what you might think about yourself, you are a good idea. God's mind thought of you, and God's Spirit brought you into being. You are the result of His idea, and that makes you very valuable to Him.

God specifically placed the woman in the garden of Eden along with the man. In Genesis 3:8, we read that God walked in the garden in the cool of the day in order to meet with Adam and Eve. The garden represents man's relationship with God, the place of fellowship.

You cannot be the kind of woman you are supposed to be if you are outside of God any more than a man can be anything outside of God. Any woman who is outside a relationship with the Lord is a dangerous woman, just as a man who is outside a relationship with the Lord is dangerous. You can be who you were created to be, and you can fulfill the purpose you were meant to fulfill, only as long as you remain in the garden of fellowship with God. Paul admonishes us in Ephesians 5:17–18, "*Therefore do not be foolish, but understand what the Lord's will is.... Be filled with the Spirit.*"

Therefore, you cannot become all of what God intends for you as a woman of purpose and power unless you are continually in fellowship with Him, filled with His Spirit, learning His will, and obeying His Word. Many women today are not living godly lives. They have rebelled against God's plan. They are living outside the garden in the wilderness. If this describes your life, return to the garden of fellowship with God today. Your heavenly Father is waiting for you. "*I will give them a heart to know me, that I am the* Lord. *They will be my people, and I will be their God, for they will return to me with all their heart*" (Jeremiah 24:7).

*Thought:* A woman cannot fulfill her purpose unless she is in relationship with God.

*Readings:* Psalm 51:1–13; 2 Peter 1:3–11

# OF THE SAME SUBSTANCE

*"Then the* L<small>ORD</small> *God made a woman from the rib he had taken out of the man, and he brought her to the man."*
—Genesis 2:22

There was beautiful structuring in the creation of the female, as well as profound meaning. When God had finished making her, she was just like the male in substance. She was so much in likeness to him that, when God presented her to him, his first words were, *"This is now bone of my bones and flesh of my flesh; she shall be called 'woman,' for she was taken out of man"* (Genesis 2:23). And the woman became his wife. The man's words are both moving and instructive. Something that is constructed has the same components as the material from which it was made. Therefore, God built the female out of the part that He took from the male so that they would be made of exactly the same substance.

The first principle to note regarding the woman is that she was created as a result of something beautiful. Woman came about because of love; it was love that caused her existence. The primary purpose of the female was to be loved by the male, just as God's major purpose for creating the spirit-man was to give him love.

God's creation of the female is fascinating because it exactly parallels His creation of man. Just as God had drawn man from Himself and created him as a spiritual being, He drew the woman out of the man and made her a physical being. God, who is love, desired someone to whom to give His love, and so He created man out of Himself. Similarly, the male needed someone to whom to give his love, and so God created the female from the male's own body. This parallel in creation illustrates the oneness and mutual love that God and man and male and female were created to have.

The word "rib" in Genesis 2:22 is the Hebrew word *tsela*. It does not necessarily mean a rib as we understand the word. It could mean "side" or "chamber." The Scripture is telling us that God drew the woman from a part of the man because the receiver has to be exactly like the giver. Just as man needed to be spirit in order to receive love from God and be in relationship with Him, the female needed to be of the same essence as the male in order to receive love from him and be in relationship with him.

Though the woman was taken from the man and was built to be like him, she is a distinct creation. This is highlighted in her physical difference from the man in that she is able to bear children. You could say that a woman is a "wombed man." She is still the same as a male, but she has certain differences. These differences are complementary in nature and are designed so that the male and female can fulfill one another's emotional and physical needs while they are spiritually nourished by God and His love, and so that together they can fulfill their purposes.

⌒

*Thought*: Male and female are of the same substance.

*Readings*: Genesis 2:21–22; Ephesians 5:28–33

# A PLACE OF GOD'S CONTINUAL PRESENCE

*"You will fill me with joy in your presence."* —Psalm 16:11

God chose a special place on the planet and put His anointing on it for the sake of man, whom He had created. First Adam, and then Eve, as well, was placed in a delightful environment—a little spot of heaven on earth. (See Genesis 2:8.)

A central reason that God placed Adam and Eve in the garden of Eden was so that they could be in His presence all the time. They could walk and talk with the Lord in the cool of the day. They could hear His voice. This was a place where communion, fellowship, and oneness with God were always intact.

A manufacturer will always position a part in the location where it can best carry out its purpose. God, as our Maker, chose the best possible location and plan for mankind. We can conclude from what we've learned about the environment of the garden that the primary purpose of man is to be in God's presence. Man is not wired to function outside the presence of the Lord.

Here's the significance: God never intended for Adam and Eve to move from the garden. He intended for the *garden to move over the earth*. God wanted them to take the presence of the garden and spread it throughout the world. This is what He meant when He told Adam and Eve to have dominion over the earth. (See Genesis 1:26–28.) This is still God's purpose. As it says in Isaiah 11:9, *"The earth will be full of the knowledge of the LORD as the waters cover the sea."* Adam and Eve could fulfill this purpose only if they were in constant communion with the God of the garden.

Likewise, to live in your purpose, you must make a decision to develop a consistent and deep relationship with God through Christ. *"Make every effort to be found spotless, blameless and at peace with him.... Grow in the grace and knowledge of our Lord and Savior Jesus Christ"* (2 Peter 3:14, 18).

⟋

*Thought* : God didn't intend for Adam and Eve to move from the garden. He intended for the garden to move over the earth.

*Readings*: Psalm 89:1–18; 1 Thessalonians 5:16–24

# KNOW YOUR IDENTITY

*"But when he, the Spirit of truth, comes, he will guide you into all the truth."*                    —John 16:13

Jesus was given to prayer and reflection during His entire earthly life. He was in constant contact with the Father in order to know how to fulfill His life's purpose. After a day of particularly busy ministry in which He had healed the sick and demon-possessed, He got up early the next day and went to pray in a quiet place. When Peter and the other disciples found Him there, they exclaimed, *"Everyone is looking for you!"* (Mark 1:37).

Jesus could have basked in the people's praise, but He continued to follow His life's purpose. God had shown Him the next step when He was in prayer. He said, *"Let us go somewhere else—to the nearby villages—so I can preach there also. That is why I have come"* (Mark 1:38).

Until you can hear the voice of God, you will be hindered in becoming a woman of purpose and power. You aren't fulfilling your purpose until you start speaking and affirming His Word in your life. To do this, you need to be in the same "garden environment" that Adam and Eve were first placed in.

We need to get back to the place where the glory can flow between God and man, where we can hear the voice of God, and God can give us direction. Because the Holy Spirit has been poured out into the hearts of believers, the garden is no longer just one spot on the earth—it is within the heart of every person who belongs to Christ. That is why Christ said, *"The kingdom of God is within you"* (Luke 17:21 NKJV). It is not within you of its own accord; the kingdom of God is within you because God's Spirit lives within you.

The kingdom of God—God's Spirit and will ruling in our hearts—has come to us through Christ, and it is through Him that we can fulfill the dominion mandate. We are called to spread the gospel message of reconciliation with God through Christ and of the gift of the Holy Spirit, who brings us power for living, working, and creating to the glory of God. If we want to fulfill our dominion responsibilities and assignments, we have to do so through the Spirit of God as we follow His will.

*Thought*: You aren't fulfilling your purpose until you can hear the voice of God and affirm His Word in your life.

*Readings*: Isaiah 11:1–5; John 14:15–26

# CREATED TO EXHIBIT GOD'S NATURE

*"The spirit of man is the candle of the* LORD.*"*
—Proverbs 20:27 (KJV)

Aprimary reason God created Adam and Eve was so that they could be in relationship with Him and continually remain in His presence. A second essential reason was so that they could reflect His character and personality. Two foundational aspects of God's character are *love* and *light,* and man (male and female) is designed to exhibit these qualities.

Man was always meant to reveal God's nature in the context of being continually connected to Him in fellowship. Jesus spoke of that connection when He referred to Himself as the Vine and us as the branches: *"I am the vine; you are the branches. If you remain in me and I in you, you will bear much fruit; apart from me you can do nothing"* (John 15:5). First John 4:16 says, *"Whoever lives in love lives in God, and God in them,"* and Proverbs 20:27 says, *"The spirit of man is the candle of the* LORD*"* (KJV). This means that when you have fellowship with God, you reflect His light. You show the nature of God, for *"God is light; in him there is no darkness at all"* (1 John 1:5).

A third reason for the creation of humanity was so that men and women could share God's authority. *"Let us make man in our image,…and let them rule* ["have dominion" NKJV, KJV]*"* (Genesis 1:26 NIV84). God never wanted to rule by Himself. Love doesn't think in those terms. You can always tell a person who is full of love. They don't want to do anything for their purposes alone. A selfish person wants all the glory, all the credit, all the recognition, all the attention, all the power, all the authority, all the rights, and all the privileges. But a person of love wants others to share in what they have.

Note again that the word *"man"* in Genesis 1:26 refers to the spirit-being created in God's image. The purpose of dominion was given to man *the spirit*. This was before the creation of male and female. Therefore, spiritually, both male and female have the same responsibility toward the earth because rule was given to the spirit-man, which resides in both of them.

Man has been given the freedom to exhibit creativity while governing the physical earth and all the other living things that dwell in it. The earth is to be ruled over, taken care of, fashioned, and molded by beings made in the image of their Creator. In this way, man is meant to reflect the loving and creative Spirit of God.

God also created man to demonstrate His wisdom and the goodness of His precepts. This purpose is part of God's eternal plans: *"His intent was that now, through the church, the manifold wisdom of God should be made known to the rulers and authorities in the heavenly realms, according to his eternal purpose that he accomplished in Christ Jesus our Lord"* (Ephesians 3:10–11).

A woman of purpose and power exhibits all of these aspects as she relies on God's Spirit to guide and enable her.

*Thought*: Spiritually, both male and female have the same responsibility toward the earth.

*Readings*: Psalm 100; John 15:5–17

— Day 24 —

# CREATED TO BE GOD'S CHILDREN

*"Giving joyful thanks to the Father, who has qualified you to share in the inheritance of his holy people in the kingdom of light."* —Colossians 1:12

When God created men and women to share His authority, it was in the context of their relationship to Him as His offspring. God didn't create us to be servants but to be children who are involved in running the "family business." This was His plan for mankind from the beginning. He has always wanted His children to help Him fulfill His purposes.

This means that God doesn't want us to work *for* Him; He wants us to work *with* Him. The Bible says that we are *"God's co-workers"* (2 Corinthians 6:1), or *"workers together with him"* (KJV). In the original Greek, *"co-workers"* means those who "cooperate," who "help with," who "work together."

It's common to hear people say, "I'm working for Jesus." If you are working *for* Jesus, you are still a hired hand. But when you understand the family business, then you become a worker alongside Christ.

What are some of the implications of our being God's children, working in His business? First, we don't have to worry about our day-to-day living expenses. If your father and mother owned a prosperous business, and they put you in charge of it, should you wonder where you will get food to eat? Should you wonder where you will get water to drink? Should you wonder where you're going to get clothes to wear? No, you are family, and you are going to be provided for. In God's company, there's always plenty of provision to go around, and you can rely on that with confidence.

Second, the Lord's directive to the male and female was, *"Fill the earth and subdue it"* (Genesis 1:28). He was telling them, in essence, "Have dominion over this spot right here so that you become used to ruling on a smaller scale at first." The implication is that He intended for this man and woman to grow in dominion ability by learning to dominate the garden of Eden, the area in which they were initially placed. This is one of God's clear principles: If you've been faithful over a little, then your rulership will be expanded to much more.

Jesus explained this concept clearly in the parable of the talents. To the servant who has been faithful over a little, the Master says, *"Well done, good and faithful servant! You have been faithful with a few things; I will put you in charge of many things. Come and share your master's happiness!"* (Matthew 25:23).

God is so good to us. He doesn't give us more than we can handle. He always gives us just enough to train us for the rest. I hope you understand this principle. God will always give you just enough so that you can get used to the idea of more. Many of us want everything right now. We short-circuit God's plan because we grasp for everything at once. God is saying, in effect, "You'll get everything, but not right at this moment. You have not yet developed the character and the experience and the exercising of your potential to enable you to handle more."

⌒

*Thought*: God always gives us just enough to train us for the rest.
*Readings*: Exodus 19:3–6; Matthew 25:14–30.

# THE SOURCE OF CONFLICT

*"Each person is tempted when they are dragged away by their own evil desire and enticed. Then, after desire has conceived, it gives birth to sin; and sin, when it is full-grown, gives birth to death."* —James 1:14–16

I f Adam and Eve were created to be in fellowship with God and one another, what happened to change this? Genesis 3 explains the initial source of the conflict between men and women. The devil, in the form of a serpent, tempted the first woman, Eve, to eat what God had forbidden her—and Adam—to eat. (See Genesis 2:16–17.) Personally, I don't think this was the first time the serpent had approached her. First, she didn't seem surprised to see him or to hear him speaking. Second, I believe they had talked earlier about God's instructions because of the way the devil phrased his crafty question: *"Did God really say, 'You must not eat from any tree in the garden'?"* (Genesis 3:1). He wanted to cast doubt on Eve's understanding of what God had said.

Eve replied, *"We may eat fruit from the trees in the garden, but God did say, 'You must not eat fruit from the tree that is in the middle of the garden, and you must not touch it, or you will die'"* (verses 2–3). She had most of her information correct, so the devil's next ploy was to try to undermine God's integrity in her eyes. *"'You will not certainly die,' the serpent said to the woman. 'For God knows that when you eat of it your eyes will be opened, and you will be like God, knowing good and evil'"* (verses 4–5).

Eve succumbed to the temptation, Adam joined her of his own free will, and they both ate of the fruit of the tree. (See verse

6.) This decision to reject God's purposes resulted in the spiritual deaths of the man and the woman. It was the beginning of the conflict between man and God and men and women that we are still dealing with today. But God had a plan of restoration.

⟋⟍

*Thought:* The devil's first tactic against human beings was to cast doubt on what God had said.

*Readings:* Genesis 3:1–7; James 1:12–18

# LOSING THE GARDEN

*"So the LORD God banished him from the Garden of Eden to work the ground from which he had been taken."*
—Genesis 3:23

Adam and Eve went against God's commandment. It was the spirit-man—the responsible spiritual being—within both the male and female that made the fateful choice to eat the fruit in disobedience to God's command. This is why mankind's ultimate dilemma is a spiritual one.

When Adam and Eve rebelled, they immediately died a spiritual death—just as God had warned—and eventually the physical houses God had given them to live in on the earth also died. However, the spiritual death was the worse predicament of the two because it separated them from their former perfect fellowship with God. God still loved them, but they no longer had the same open channel to Him with which to receive His love. While they still retained elements of their creation in God's image, they no longer perfectly reflected the nature and character of their Creator.

The devil had presented Adam and Eve with a big lie, and they had fallen for it, to their own sorrow. However, there was an underlying reason that mankind fell. To understand it, we need to return to two foundational principles of purpose: (1) To discover the purpose of something, never ask the creation; ask the creator. (2) We find our purpose only in the mind of our Maker. Adam and Eve stopped looking to their Creator for their purpose and instead looked to themselves. In doing so, they lost their ability to fulfill their true purpose.

In the broken relationship between Adam and Eve and the cursed ground that followed their sin (see Genesis 3:14–19), we see Satan's scheme to undermine God's purposes of dominion. Satan was afraid of the power that would be released through a man and woman united in God's purposes. Therefore, he sought to distort the relationship between males and females and limit the garden of Eden by bringing an atmosphere of thorns and thistles to the rest of the earth.

Yet, even though Adam and Eve fell, God's purpose for humanity has never changed. At the very hour of humanity's rejection of His purpose, God promised a Redeemer who would save men and woman from their fallen state and all its ramifications. (See Genesis 3:15.) The Redeemer would restore the relationship and partnership of males and females. Jesus Christ is that Redeemer and, because of Him, men and women can return to God's original design for them. We can fulfill His purposes once again. We can have true dominion over the earth—but only through Christ.

⌒

*Thought:* Satan was afraid of the power that would be released through a man and woman united in God's purposes.

*Readings:* Genesis 3:8–24; Romans 5:12–21

# LIFE IS PRECIOUS

*"Above all else, guard your heart, for everything you do flows from it."* —Proverbs 4:23

When Adam and Eve turned their backs on God and His ways, they ended up losing their knowledge of His intent for themselves and for the world. Rejecting God was the equivalent of buying a sophisticated and intricate piece of equipment and then throwing away the user's manual. If you get something to work under those circumstances, it is only by chance. The more likely scenario is that you will never get it to function properly. It will never fulfill its complete purpose.

Likewise, humanity has not respected the fact that God's creation and His directions for living were established for a specific reason. If that purpose continues to be abandoned, women and men will never function properly as human beings. This dangerous situation leads to us back to one of the key principles for understanding life and relationships: *whenever purpose is not known, abuse is inevitable.*

Life is too valuable to be treated like a trial run. It's a dangerous thing for us to experiment with this precious commodity. In the Psalms, we are reminded that God's Manual, the Word, directs our way: *"Your word is a lamp for my feet, a light on my path"* (Psalm 119:105). *"Your statutes [Word] are my heritage forever; they are the joy of my heart"* (verse 111). *"The unfolding of your words gives light; it gives understanding to the simple"* (verse 130). If we look to ourselves or others, rather than to God and His Manual, to learn our reason for living, we will travel an unreliable and hazardous course in life.

What value do you place on your life? Do you know that one of the most dangerous things in life is wasting time? It is said that time is a commodity that you never are able to recapture. Once you've lost time, it's gone forever. So the best thing to do with time is to use it in a way that will bring the greatest results. The best way—the only way—to use time effectively is to do *what* you are supposed to do *when* you are supposed to do it. Effectiveness does not mean just doing good things but rather doing the *right* thing.

⌒

*Thought*: You have to make your life count if you are ever to fulfill your purpose.

*Readings*: Proverbs 4:18–27; Hebrews 4:12–16

# RESTORED BY REDEMPTION

*"For he has rescued us from the dominion of darkness and brought us into the kingdom of the Son he loves, in whom we have redemption, the forgiveness of sins."*

—Colossians 1:13–14

Jesus Christ restored humanity to God's purpose and plan. I define the plan of God very simply. The first two chapters of Genesis are a depiction of God's perfect program for the spirit-man and his manifestation as male and female. Chapter 3 of Genesis reveals how and why this program fell apart. Genesis 3 to Revelation 21, the last chapter of the Bible, explain what God has done and is still doing to restore humanity to His original program (and even beyond). The Bible is an account of God's restoration program, which He effected through various covenants with His people.

Christ's life, death, and resurrection accomplished the redemption of man. The sacrifice of the perfect Man made atonement for the sins of fallen man and restored humanity to the fellowship with God it had enjoyed in the garden of Eden. This means that the curse of sin is removed from people's lives when they receive Christ's redemptive work and are born again. Christ's own Spirit comes to dwell within them, they are restored to God's purposes, and they are able to love and serve God again.

Under the redemptive work of Christ, the woman is restored not only to fellowship with God, but also to the position of partner with her male counterpart. Therefore, she is not to be dominated or ruled by the male, because, if she were, it would mean that the redemptive work of Christ had not been successful.

Jesus said, "*When the Advocate* [Holy Spirit] *comes, whom I will send to you from the Father—the Spirit of truth who goes out from the Father—he will testify about me. And you also must testify, for you have been with me from the beginning*" (John 15:26–27). From the Father *through* the Son *by* the Spirit, we are taught the truth, which we, in turn, teach others. This is part of man's dominion assignment carried out by redeemed men and women. The only instruction we are supposed to speak comes from the Father. The Father, through Jesus, gives instructions by the Holy Spirit to the bride, the church. Then the church takes the instructions from her Lord and speaks them out with authority as commands. This is the principle behind Jesus's statements to believers regarding authority. He has given His Bride, the church, the authority to use His name to command sickness, disease, demons, and mountains. (See Luke 9:1–2; Matthew 17:20; Mark 16:17–18.)

As the bride of Christ, the church has the Father's instruction, authority, and power to speak and act with boldness in the world. The church binds, looses, heals, and delivers under the authority of our Teacher and Husband, Jesus Christ. (See, for example, Matthew 16:19.)

⌒

*Thought*: Under the redemptive work of Christ, the woman is restored not only to fellowship with God, but also to the position of partner with her male counterpart.

*Readings*: Psalm 107; Revelation 5:9–10

# BECOMING A WHOLE PERSON

*"Seek first his kingdom and his righteousness, and all these things will be given to you as well."* —Matthew 6:33

We have seen that when a man falls in love with God's presence, he begins to function as he was meant to. When a man wants to marry you, do not ask him if he loves you; ask him if he loves God. If his love for God is not his first priority, then he is a poor prospect for a fulfilling, lasting relationship.

Refuse to form relationships with plastic men who melt when the heat and pressures of life get turned up high. Find someone who is real. Until you find a man who knows that God the Father is his Source and Sustainer, you must lean on Jesus. He will husband you until you find a man who can be a godly husband and father.

Some single women are afraid of being unmarried and alone. When they hit age twenty-five, thirty, or thirty-five, they begin to think they're past their prime, and so they say to themselves, "I'm never going to get married. I'd better latch onto the first thing that comes along." That's the reason many people marry spouses who aren't right for them. The problem is that they haven't yet learned what it means to be a whole person.

There is a difference between "being alone" and "being lonely." You can be lonely in a crowd of people, and you can be alone and still happy as a lark. There is nothing wrong with being alone at times. The Bible tells us that it's important to be alone and quiet before the Lord. Jesus often made a point to go off by Himself in order to pray and rest. Many people don't have time for God because they're too busy trying to find a mate.

Being alone can be healthy—but loneliness is like a disease. Jesus talked about the attitude we should have when He said, in effect, "Don't worry about what you're going to eat, what you're going to wear, or whom you're going to marry. Seek first the kingdom of God. Become immersed in His righteousness. Then God will meet all your needs." (See Matthew 6:31–33.)

The criteria for marriage is not merely being old enough, but also whether or not it will be beneficial. (See 1 Corinthians 6:12.) If you don't have a clear understanding of the purpose of marriage, it's not going to benefit you. If your potential spouse doesn't have a clear understanding of who he or she is in Christ and who males and females were created to be, it will not be beneficial for you.

The first man, Adam, was so busy following the command of God that, when his mate, Eve, came along, he was ready, and it was the right time for him. (See Genesis 2:15–25.) Stay in the garden of God's righteousness because, if it's His will for you to have a spouse, you will need to understand His ways if you want that relationship to be a good one.

Follow God's purpose and you will avoid heartache and regret in your relationships, because His purpose is the key to your fulfillment.

⌒

*Thought*: Be prepared for meeting your spouse by first understanding and obeying God's ways.

*Readings*: Deuteronomy 6:5; Matthew 6:25–33

# — Day 30 —
# THE FOUNDATION OF
# THE FAMILY

*"The LORD God formed a man from the dust of the ground and breathed into his nostrils the breath of life, and the man became a living being."* —Genesis 2:7

When you think about it, God really made only one human being. When He created the female, He didn't go back to the soil, but He fashioned her from the side of the man. (See Genesis 2:21–23.) Only the male came directly from the earth. This was because the male was designed by God to be the foundation of the human family. The woman came out of the man rather than the earth because she was designed to rest on the man—to have the male as her support.

God planned everything before He created it, and He started with the foundation. Have you ever seen a contractor build a house starting with the roof? No. Likewise, you don't start with the windows. You don't start with the gutters or the rafters. God starts like any other builder. The priority in building is always what you need to do first. You begin with the foundation.

I believe that the foundation of society, the infrastructure God intended for this world, has been misunderstood. We often say that the family is the foundation of society. It is very true that the family is the adhesive that holds it together. Yet God did not start to build earthly society with a family. He began it with one person. He began it with the male.

Yet we must remember that even though the male is the foundation of the family, men and women were created equal. *"In Christ Jesus you are all children of God through faith.... There is neither Jew* nor Gentile, slave nor free, nor is there male and female, for you are all one in Christ Jesus" (Galatians 3:26, 28). Men and women are equal. That's not for a senate or a congress or a cabinet or a parliament of any nation to decide. God already made this decision in creation! Then He reaffirmed it with the redemption of mankind in Jesus Christ. Male and female are one in Christ. Don't ever give anybody the right to say what kind of human value you have. Don't let anybody else tell you how much of a person you are. When you understand that equality is inherent in creation and discover how it is to be manifested in your life, then you can begin to live in the full realm of that equality, regardless of what others might tell you about yourself.

~

*Thought*: While the male is the foundation of the human family, men and women were created equal.

*Readings*: Genesis 2:4–23; 1 Corinthians 11:3, 7–12

# DISTINCT,
# NOT SUPERIOR OR INFERIOR

*"Heirs with you of the gracious gift of life."*     —1 Peter 3:7

Today, many of those who advocate equal rights say that there is no difference at all between women and men. Yet while women and men were created equal, they were also created distinct. This is part of their unique design. This statement may confuse some people and anger others, because somehow we have come to believe that *different* means *inferior* or *superior*. Don't confuse being different with being either lesser or greater. Different does not imply inferiority or superiority; different simply means different. This is especially true in regard to men and women; their differences are necessary because of their purposes.

In many spheres of life, we don't consider differences to be weaknesses but rather mutual strengths. In music, who is more important to a full symphony orchestra, a violin player or an oboe player? Both work together in harmony. In sports, who is more important to a swimming medley relay, the swimmer who swims the breaststroke or the swimmer who swims the backstroke? Both have to be strong swimmers in their particular specialties, because a medley race cannot be swum with only one type of swimmer. When they win, they share the honor together.

The answer to the historical devaluing of women does not lie in declaring that there are no differences between females and males, but in recognizing and affirming their complementary differences. We must understand and accept these differences so they can be used in harmony, like a finely tuned orchestra.

God's intent that women be equal heirs with men in creation and redemption remains largely an ignored truth. Men's internal devaluing of women is the reason women generally continue to be discounted and exploited in almost every society in the world, regardless of recent social and political advances. In developed nations as well as developing nations, the plight of the female is still very real. It is tragic to have to admit this is true in our modern society.

Many women are involved in opportunities and activities that were formerly reserved for males, such as leadership, management, and sports. However, although we can say that there has been some improvement, in most societies, women are still suffering the prejudice of the male against the female. Men's hearts cannot be changed by legislation. Even though the law now says, "Women are equal to men," this doesn't mean that men think so. The persistent devaluing of women continues to hold back progress, and women are being treated in every way *except* in the way God originally intended: *"heirs with you of the gracious gift of life."* Through God's grace, we can restore the relationships between women and men and fulfill God's original purposes for mankind.

∽

*Thought*: God's intent that women be equal heirs with men in creation and redemption remains largely an ignored truth.

*Readings*: Genesis 2:26–28; 1 Peter 3:1–7

# JESUS SUBMITTED TO
# THE FATHER

"[Jesus] *did not consider equality with God something to be used to his own advantage; rather, he made himself nothing by taking the very nature of a servant.*" —Philippians 2:6–7

Man did not come from woman, but woman from man" (1 Corinthians 11:8). The entire eleventh chapter of 1 Corinthians talks about the position of men and women and about the male-female relationship. It talks about authority.

Some people feel that Paul was being a chauvinist when he made the above statement. Rather, he was referring to the creation of male and female. He made an important distinction between the spiritual position of men and women and the male-female relationship. In doing so, he used a spiritual example because he did not want his statements to be misinterpreted.

Paul was saying, in effect, "Look, some of you women think that I am trying to put you down or say that you are inferior. Therefore, in order to make myself clear, let me explain to both men and women the true nature of authority." In 1 Corinthians 11:3, Paul said, "*Now I want you to realize that the head of every man is Christ.*" So first we see that the man has a head to whom he is responsible. He is under the headship of Christ. Verse three continues, "*And the head of the woman is man.*" The woman also has a head. She is responsible to the man. The verse concludes, "*And the head of Christ is God.*" Paul was expressing this idea: "If you think you don't like being under somebody else's authority, you will have to tell Jesus to move out from under the Father's authority. Until you become better than Jesus, the best thing to do is to stay under your authority."

There is an evil spirit abroad in the world today in which nobody wants to be under anybody else. This satanic spirit has taken over our society. Yet Jesus Himself gave us our model of authority and submission when He submitted to His Father. Philippians 2:6–8 says:

[Jesus] *being in very nature God, did not consider equality with God something to be used to his own advantage; rather, he made himself nothing by taking the very nature of a servant, being made in human likeness. And being found in appearance as a man, he humbled himself by becoming obedient to death—even death on a cross!*

Even though Jesus is equal to God, He submitted Himself to the Father and to the Father's plan.

A woman may be smarter, have more education, work a more prestigious job, or make more money than her husband. Yet for him to fulfill his role, she needs to submit to him. Submission is an act of the will, a choice. A woman should submit to her husband, not because the man says so, and not because society says so, but because of her purpose. In this way, she enables her husband to be a leader.

⌣

*Thought*: Jesus Himself gave us our model of authority and submission when He submitted to His Father.

*Readings*: Isaiah 53; Philippians 2:5–11

# SUBMISSION ACTIVATES HEAVEN

*"A man ought not to cover his head, since he is the image and glory of God; but the woman is the glory of man."*
—1 Corinthians 11:7

In our opening verse, above, Paul was saying that once the man is covered with Christ, his marriage is under authority. However, the woman then needs the man to cover her. First Corinthians 11:9–10 says, *"Neither was man created for woman, but woman for man. For this reason, and because of the angels, the woman ought to have a sign of authority on her head"* (NIV84).

If you are a woman who wants to do a work for God, all of heaven is ready to work for you. God says, "All right, we'll do spiritual work, but how are your relationships in the natural realm? What is your relationship with your husband, your family members, the members of your church?" Any woman who says, "I don't need the church; I can do this by myself," isn't going to find any angels supporting her. The angels are looking for your authority. They will ask, "Whom are you under? How can you expect us to help you under God's authority when you yourself aren't under anybody?" Submission activates heaven.

Now, if Christ submitted to the Father, who do we think we are? You may be independent, famous, a fantastic businessperson, and doing very well. However, if you aren't going to submit to anyone, heaven won't trust you. Don't believe that you can run off and do God's work without being in submission. Don't ever run away from a ministry and do your own work because somebody there made you upset. The angels are watching. You may actually remove God's protective covering from yourself when you move out from under your authority. This spiritual principle applies to both males and females.

Yet here's what most people forget when it comes to submission: men and women are created to be *inter*dependent. *"In the Lord, however, woman is not independent of man, nor is man independent of woman"* (1 Corinthians 11:11 NIV84). God is saying, in effect, "Men and women need one another. They need each other to be complete."

*"For as woman came from man, so also man is born of woman"* (verse 12). I like that statement. Men need women to give birth to them, but women need men to enable them to conceive. This is definitely not an inferiority-superiority situation. It has to do with complementary purposes. Ephesians 5, which talks about wives submitting to their husbands, also says, "Submit to one another *out of reverence for Christ"* (verse 21). There has to be a mutual submitting to one another if God's purposes are to be carried out on the earth.

⌒

*Thought*: If you won't submit to anyone, heaven won't trust you.

*Readings*: Judges 4:1–5:9; Romans 16:1–15

# THE ESSENCE OF THE MATTER

*"In the Lord woman is not independent of man, nor is man independent of woman. For as woman came from man, so also man is born of woman. But everything comes from God."*
—1 Corinthians 11:11–12

Everything comes full circle. After all that Paul had taught—that woman came from man and was created for man—he then placed both male and female in the same spiritual position.

My wife and I are equal before the Lord. She can go before the Lord and get the same spiritual help that I get. She doesn't need to go through me, her husband. That is why, if you are a single mother, your spirit can go to God and do business with Him. You don't need to get permission from a man to go to God; you have a spirit-man within. *The essence of the matter is this:* in the spiritual realm, there is no difference between men and women, but in the physical realm, there has to be the proper relationship of submission.

Once, I was speaking to a woman who is in management at an insurance company. She told me, "You know, at work, I'm the boss. Yet when I walk through the door into my home, I'm a wife." That's a smart woman. Of course, you can be the boss at work. But when you get home, you're a wife, and your husband is your head, or authority. That means you can't treat your husband like one of your employees at the office. An altogether different authority takes over. Yet a husband has to understand that he is supposed to be in the Lord when he's in the home, and that he himself is under God's authority.

*Thought*: In the spiritual realm, there is no difference between men and women, but in the physical realm, there has to be the proper relationship of submission.

*Readings*: 2 Samuel 22:26–28; Ephesians 5:21–25

# FALSE SUBMISSION

*"Therefore do not be foolish, but understand what the Lord's will is."* —Ephesians 5:17

Dealing with submission in a situation where a woman has an unbelieving husband can be difficult, but the Bible gives us guidelines for what to do under these circumstances. First Corinthians 7 says that if a woman holds to the standards of the Word of God and her unbelieving husband agrees to stay with her, *"let her not leave him"* (verse 13 KJV). However, if he cannot live with her convictions, the Scripture says, *"Let him depart"* (verse 15 KJV). In other words, if he can't live with her commitment to the Lord, the Bible tells her, "Let him go." You don't compromise your faith, even for your spouse.

Some women have a false view of submission. They allow their husbands to beat them half to death because they think that is being submissive. I have counseled many women who think this way. They come to my office badly battered and ask, "What am I supposed to do?" I say, "Remove yourself from the premises." "But the Bible says to submit." "Yes, but not to a beating. You are to submit to the Lord. Until you see the Lord in the house, leave. You are not to be foolish enough just to sit there and let your life be put in jeopardy."

There is nothing in the Bible that says a woman should agree to do something that's against God's Word or allow herself to suffer abuse. First Peter 2:19–20 says that if you suffer for the sake of the gospel, that is true suffering. But if you suffer for the sake of your own sin and folly, that is not to your credit. It's foolish for you to let somebody beat you black and blue and then turn around and say, "It's all for Jesus." That is not submission. You need to protect yourself.

⌒

*Thought*: There is nothing in the Bible that says a woman should allow herself to suffer abuse.

*Readings*: Proverbs 2:1–15; 1 Corinthians 7:10–17

# WOMAN AS ENHANCER

*"The Lord God said, 'It is not good for the man to be alone.
I will make a helper suitable for him.'"* —Genesis 2:18

Although the male was created first and was given the role of foundation and responsible spiritual leader, the female is a coleader as an enhancer. She shares his vision and works with him to accomplish what they were both created to do. The woman takes who the man is and what the man has and enlarges and extends it. In this way, his leadership is effective and their shared vision becomes reality.

A good illustration of this is the relationship between Jesus and His church. Jesus is called the Head, and the church is called the body. (See Colossians 1:18.) They work in unison with one another. Christ's relationship to the church is the perfect model for us of the male-female relationship and God's purposes for the woman in her dominion leadership role.

God always tells you why He makes something before He makes it. *"The Lord God said, 'It is not good for the man to be alone. I will make a helper suitable for him.'"* It is clear that, when God made this statement, He meant that what He was about to create for Adam would be good for him. Therefore, God's Word affirms, "Women are good. Females are good." The woman was created for the man's good.

The first purpose of the female as enhancer is to be a companion for the male, so that he won't be alone. The word *alone* is made up of two words, "all" and "one." When you put these words together, you see that *alone* basically means "all in one."

God said, "It is not good for this male to be all in one, having everything in himself." God made the female so that the male would have someone to give to, someone to share his vision with, someone to be a part of his life. Isn't it sad that many men don't see women in this way? The female was created so that the male would not have to be alone. She is his life companion. "To companion" means to accompany, to attend, and even to guide someone. It is in this sense that a woman is a man's companion.

Thought: The woman shares the man's vision and works with him to accomplish what they were both created to do.

Readings: 2 Kings 4:8–36; Acts 18:1–4, 18–19, 24–28

# CREATED TO BE A HELPMATE

*"I will make a helper suitable for him."* —Genesis 2:18

In God's wisdom, if a woman is *meant* to be a helper, she has been designed with many qualities and abilities that *equip her to help.* Remember that the Creator always has a plan for His creations.

A wife's purpose is to assist her husband in fulfilling God's plan for his life. The implications of this are profound. First, it means the male has to have a plan; otherwise, the female is in trouble. The world is filled with frustrated women who live with men who aren't going anywhere. The first question a woman should ask a man after he proposes is, "Where are you going in life?" If he can't answer this question, she should tell him to find a map and say that she'll talk to him later. A woman is too valuable a person to waste sitting in a house being frustrated for twenty years. It breaks my heart to see the precious, awesome potential of a female being suffocated by some male who doesn't know what he's doing.

Second, it means that the female must understand that her fulfillment is related to the male's vision. In other words, she can never really be complete if she does not help him fulfill his vision.

When a wife decides she wants a completely different vision for her life than her husband's vision, they will experience a division. *Di* means two or double. The word *division* could be thought of as "double vision." Whenever you have a couple who has double vision, they are in danger of divorce because *"a house divided against itself will fall"* (Luke 11:17). You can't have two visions in the same household, or the man and the woman will be going in different directions. That is why God created the woman to be in a helping position. Helpers don't take over; rather, they assist. This certainly does not mean that a woman should not have her own interests and develop her own abilities. It means that, as a couple, they need to share the same vision for their lives.

*If you have any encouragement from being united with Christ, if any comfort from his love, if any common sharing in the Spirit, if any tenderness and compassion, then make my joy complete by being like-minded, having the same love, being one in spirit and of one mind. Do nothing out of selfish ambition or vain conceit. Rather, in humility value others above yourselves, not looking to your own interests but each of you to the interests of the others.* (Philippians 2:1–4)

*Thought*: You can't have two visions in the same household, or the man and the woman will be going in different directions.

*Readings*: Psalm 133:1; John 17:20–23

# USING YOUR GIFTS TO HELP

*"Each of you should use whatever gift you have received to serve others, as faithful stewards of God's grace in its various forms."* —1 Peter 4:10

God has given women many wonderful gifts, and He says, in effect, "I gave you all these things not only for your own enrichment and enjoyment, but also so that you can use these gifts in your position as coleader and helper with men."

If you are a woman, how are you using your gifts? You may be talented, educated, experienced, eloquent, and well dressed. Are you using these assets to prove to men that you are just as good as they are? That's not a help; that's competition. God's plan is for men and women to work together for mutual benefit.

Women often need to exercise special wisdom when helping men, however, because the last thing many men want to admit is that they *need* help. They don't understand how God has designed women to help them. When a woman tries to assist a man, therefore, the man may interpret her help as nagging. For example, a woman may be trying to say to her husband, "God's vision is for you to be the spiritual leader for me and for our children; however, you can't be a spiritual leader if you won't develop your spiritual life." So, the next day, she asks, "When are we going to pray?" He retorts, "Don't bother me right now. The Lord will tell me when to pray."

The man needs to appreciate the woman's role of helper, and the woman needs discernment when giving help. If the man messes up or fails, the woman shouldn't kick him when he's down.

Helpers pick people up and dust them off. Do you know how many men are where they are today because their helpers made sure they got there? Your man might not yet be the best husband, he might not yet be spiritually mature, but encourage him and help him to become all God created him to be.

~

*Thought*: How are you using your gifts?

*Readings*: Exodus 35:4–29; 2 Corinthians 13:11

# A GOOD WORD FROM A GOOD WOMAN

*"A word fitly spoken is like apples of gold in settings of silver."*
—Proverbs 25:11 (NKJV)

When God said He would make a helper for the man, I believe that He intended the woman to be the *"help meet"* (Genesis 2:18 KJV) for men in general, not just for her husband. This means that, as a woman, you are meant to be a spiritual help and encouragement to the men you encounter in life.

Please understand that I am certainly not saying a woman should submit to other men as she submits to her husband; rather, I am saying that she can be a tremendous influence for good in men's lives. Moreover, the helping nature of a woman can be exercised whether a woman is married or single, since it is a natural part of her makeup. Single women have male relatives and friends who need encouragement. A single woman has much to contribute in this way, and, if she marries, she can bring into her marriage this valuable experience of exercising her gift and understanding the nature and needs of men.

If a woman sees a man she knows destroying his life with drugs, she might go to him and say, "God has put so much potential inside of you. It breaks my heart to see you on drugs." Saying that may help him. You don't have to be married to give that type of help. Some men just need a good word from a good woman. They have been told negative things about themselves all their lives. They are looking for a woman to tell them something positive about themselves.

Let me caution you that this can require careful discretion on the woman's part so that the wrong impression is not given. Yet a woman can be a powerful force for good in a man's life by being a spiritual encouragement to him.

*Thought*: The helping nature of a woman can be exercised whether a woman is married or single, since it is a natural part of her makeup.

*Readings*: Isaiah 50:4; Colossians 4:6

# THE WOMAN'S SOURCE
# AND PROVIDER

*"Look at the birds of the air; they do not sow or reap or store
away in barns, and yet your heavenly Father feeds them. Are
you not much more valuable than they?"* —Matthew 6:26

A woman's ultimate Source and Provider is God, and she can
always turn to Him. But God has designed things so that the
female can receive earthly provision through the male. *"Man did
not come from woman, but woman from man"* (1 Corinthians 11:8)
means that the man is responsible for the woman because she came
from man. This is God's original plan.

Now, if a man starts thinking that this is *his* plan, rather than
God's, his responsibility for the woman will turn into domination
over her. We have to understand that the female's provision by the
male is God's design, or we will misuse and abuse it.

The man is responsible for providing because of his position in
the relationship of things. There is a parallel to this in the spiritual
realm. Spiritually, we are to go to God for what we need. Jesus has
told us, "Remain in Me and I will remain in you. If you are separated from Me, you can't do anything. I am the Vine; you are the
branches, which receive nourishment from the Vine." (See John
15:4–5.)

God says that the woman should remain connected to her
source. She should be able to go to the man to get answers. If you
are a married woman, and you have a question, ask your husband.
If he doesn't have the answer, then go to the next man who is in
godly authority. This also applies to a woman who is not married.
The man could be your father, your pastor, or your big brother in

the Lord, as long as it is someone who represents God as source and provider. That person should be able to give you guidance. The woman is always supposed to be able to go to her source to receive whatever she needs.

⌒

*Thought*: A woman's ultimate Source and Provider is God, and she can always turn to Him.

*Readings*: 2 Kings 4:1–7; 1 Timothy 5:3–16

# WOMAN AS REFLECTOR

*"Woman is the glory of man."*        —1 Corinthians 11:7

Several times in Ephesians 5, Paul exhorted men to love their wives: *"Husbands, love your wives, just as Christ loved the church and gave himself up for her.... Husbands ought to love their wives as their own bodies. He who loves his wife loves himself.... Each one of you also must love his wife as he loves himself"* (Ephesians 5:25, 28, 33).

When God made woman, He drew her out of man so that the man would have someone to love who was of his own nature. In this way, the man was created to be a giver of love and the woman to be a receiver of love.

In order to be fulfilled, the woman needs love. What this means is that God has designed the woman to operate on love and to reflect the love she receives. If you don't give her the love God meant for her to receive, she can't fully function in the way God created her to function.

When a woman is loved, she is better able to live a life of joy and peace, even in the midst of difficult circumstances. When she is unloved, it is as if there is a weight on her heart. *"Husbands, love your wives and do not be harsh with them"* (Colossians 3:19). Any man who violates a woman's need for love is misusing and abusing God's purpose for the woman.

It is interesting to note that nowhere in the Bible does God tell the woman to love the man. The woman is instructed to submit to the man, to respect and to honor him. Yet God commands the man over and over again to love the woman. Why? It is because the fall damaged the male's God-given natural love for the female, so that he wants to rule over her rather than to love her as himself. This is why, as the male is being restored to God's original design through redemption in Christ, he needs to be instructed to love the woman. For the same reason, the female's God-given natural respect for the male was damaged, and that is why she needs to be instructed to respect him. Thus, when God's purposes are restored, peace is reestablished between males and females; however, when the fallen nature is allowed free reign, there is discord.

When Paul said, *"Husbands, love your wives,"* he was saying, in effect, "Husband, above all else, love your wife. Don't worry about other things before that, because you can take care of those things in due course. If you love her, you will take care of many other problems and potential problems in your marriage. When you give her the love she needs, she will function properly, because she was born to be loved."

*Thought*: The primary purpose of the female's receiving nature is to receive love.

*Readings*: Proverbs 27:19; 2 Corinthians 3:17–18

# REFLECTING THE LORD'S GLORY

*"And we all, who with unveiled faces contemplate the Lord's glory, are being transformed into his image with ever-increasing glory, which comes from the Lord, who is the Spirit."*

—2 Corinthians 3:18

Jesus has a bride who is meant to reflect His nature. In the original Greek, her name is *ecclesia*. The English translation of this word is "church." Jesus sent the church into the world to be a reflection of Himself. He said to His Father, *"I have given them* [the church] *the glory that you gave me, that they may be one as we are one"* (John 17:22). Jesus said to His bride, "The world will know who I am and that I was sent by the Father by the way in which you act, by your unity with one another. The world isn't going to come to Me to find out what I'm like; the world is going to come to the bride. If you don't love one another, they'll never know what I'm like." (See John 13:34–35.)

It has often been said that a marriage is a church within the church. If the world isn't seeing the nature of Christ through the church in the way that it should, perhaps we should begin to correct this problem by first looking at the relationships between husbands and wives, fathers and daughters, brothers and sisters in our homes. We should then look at the nature of the relationships between men and women in the church.

The woman's role as reflector of the man's love and nature can powerfully reveal God's remarkable love for humanity. She can show her family, her community, and the world what it means to be loved by God and to bear the image of the Creator. She can be a witness to the world of God's compassion and sacrifice for man, and of the joy and healing we can receive through His love.

Jesus said to His disciples of those in the world who are lost, "*Open your eyes and look at the fields! They are ripe for harvest*" (John 4:35). If men and women realize the powerful impact of their relationships on the salvation of the world, they will prayerfully and seriously consider how the dominion mandate can be fulfilled as they give and reflect God's love and nature in their day-to-day relationships.

⌒

*Thought*: Jesus sent the church into the world to be a reflection of Himself.

*Readings*: Isaiah 58: 6–8; Ephesians 2:19–22

# RESPECTING AND
# AFFIRMING WOMEN

*"Husbands, in the same way be considerate as you live with
your wives, and treat them with respect."*      —1 Peter 3:7

H*usbands, love your wives, just as Christ also loved the church
and gave Himself for her, that He might sanctify...her"* (Ephesians
5:25–26 NKJV). If a man is going to love his wife, he has to keep
company with Christ. He has to find out how Christ loved His
church. It will take a lifetime to study that manual on love! He
*"gave Himself for her."* Then He sanctified her.

To sanctify something means to take it away from all else,
set it apart in a special place, care for it every day, and value it
as a priceless gem. To sanctify something means that you do not
allow anything near it that would hurt or destroy it. It is set apart
for special use. This means that you don't pass it around. It is not
available to entertain other people.

When a man really loves his wife, he considers her the crème
de la crème. When she receives such love, she will reflect it in her
countenance, the way she looks at life, and in her interactions with
others.

These principles of a woman's need to receive love have
mainly been expressed in the setting of the marriage relationship.
However, they can be more broadly applied. Just as we talked
about how women can be a spiritual help and encouragement not
only to their husbands but also to other men they encounter in
their lives, men can do the same for women. They can help build a
woman's self-esteem by valuing her and treating her with kindness
and Christian love. Women need the affirmation of men, just as

men need the respect of women. This is particularly important for men to understand, since they are often in positions in authority over women—in the church, in the workplace, and in other realms of life—and they influence their perspectives and attitudes.

We can turn to 1 Corinthians 13 as the man's guide to respecting and affirming women in any interaction or relationship he has with them. Men need to remember that females who are under their authority or supervision need to be treated with consideration so that the nature that God has given them will not be quenched. Women often reflect the manner in which they are treated by men; if men reflect the love and nature of Christ in their dealings with women, the women also can reflect the love and nature of Christ.

If you are a mother, grandmother, or aunt, or have another role of guidance or influence in a young man's life, you can teach them these principles, which will prepare them for their own marriage and interactions with women in all areas of their life.

⌒

*Thought*: Women need the affirmation of men, just as men need the respect of women.

*Readings*: Psalm 86:15; 1 Corinthians 13

# WOMAN AS LIFE-GIVER

*"Adam named his wife Eve, because she would become the mother of all the living."* —Genesis 3:20

It has been said that the pressure exerted on a woman's body during delivery would kill a man. Apparently, the pressure is so strong that a male's body could not physically hold up under it. This phenomenon sheds new meaning on the verse, *"I praise you because I am fearfully and wonderfully made; your works are wonderful, I know that full well"* (Psalm 139:14). When God created the woman to be able to carry a baby to term and to deliver that baby, He gave her extraordinary capabilities! He built her so that she could do what He had designed her to do. The woman was designed to be able to gestate—to conceive, carry a baby to term, and bring forth this new life into the world.

After the fall of humanity, but apparently before the man and woman were banished from the garden, the man gave the woman a name. *"Adam named his wife Eve, because she would become the mother of all the living"* (Genesis 3:20). The name *Eve* in the Hebrew is *Chavvah*, and it means "life-giver." It is significant that God did not cause the man and woman to leave the garden before Eve was named. Her ability to bear children, her role of life-giver, was part of God's original design and is not a result of the fall in any way.

In the month of May, the United States and other countries celebrate Mother's Day. This is appropriate for a number of reasons, but certainly so because the woman is in essence a life-giver. She was given the ability to receive the seed of the male and to reproduce after their kind. This is an awesome capability. God gave the female a powerful responsibility in the world.

Pregnancy is a remarkable process that shifts the focus and effort of the woman's entire body to the task of developing the new life within her womb. Yet the woman's dominion role of life-giver is not limited to carrying and delivering a human child. God's design for the woman as life-giver goes beyond her physical abilities. It permeates her entire makeup as a female, a theme we will explore further in the next two devotionals.

*Thought*: God gave the female the powerful responsibility of being a life-giver.

*Readings*: Genesis 17:15–22; 21:1–7; Luke 1:1–66

# THE "INCUBATOR": TRANSFORMATION AND MULTIPLICATION

*"Give, and it will be given to you. A good measure, pressed down, shaken together and running over, will be poured into your lap. For with the measure you use, it will be measured to you."* —Luke 6:38

With her life-giving capacity, we could call the woman an "incubator," because her very nature reflects her inclination to develop and give new life to things. Since God created the woman's gestational ability as an integral part of her nature, this ability permeates all areas of her life. She has a physical womb, but she also has an emotional "womb," a mental and instinctual "womb," and a spiritual "womb." She brings forth life in all these areas of her makeup. She receives things into herself, nurtures them until they mature, and then gives them back in fully developed form.

Everything goes back to the purpose and design of God. The woman's nature is to be a receiver, and that is why she can receive the seed of the man in order to create a new human life. Yet it is not only a matter of receiving, but also of being able to transform what she has received in a remarkable way, that makes her an incubator. A womb will never give back to you just what it has received. It will always take what you have given it and multiply it.

As part of her dominion role, the woman is meant to conceive, develop, and give new life to or "incubate" what she receives into herself. She is gifted with many creative abilities that can assist her loved ones, herself, and the world. When a woman receives an idea and incubates it, therefore, it becomes something greater—something bigger, stronger, and more dynamic. A woman incubates in these ways:

- ✦ She sees possibilities and potential.
- ✦ She ponders words, actions, and relationships between things.
- ✦ She processes words, ideas, needs, and problems.
- ✦ She conceives and invents.
- ✦ She develops ideas, plans, and programs.
- ✦ She protects what she has received while it develops.
- ✦ She produces something new from what she receives.
- ✦ She multiplies what she is given.

You could say that the woman is an entire research and development department all in one. In this, she reflects the nature of her Creator. Just as God created man out of Himself, a woman brings forth new life from within herself.

Many women have been so beaten down by life that they have rarely used their gifts of incubation. They have been told by others that they have nothing to contribute. I believe that God wants to set you free to develop the gifts He has placed within you and the ideas and visions He will give you. Don't be afraid. God has given you tremendous ability, and you can be a blessing to many as you reflect the nature of your Creator, the Life-Giver.

⟱

*Thought*: Whatever you give a woman, she's going to multiply it.

*Readings*: Psalm 92:4–5; John 8:36

# A SPIRITUAL INCUBATOR

*"And there was a widow in that town who kept coming to him
with the plea, 'Grant me justice against my adversary.'"*
—Luke 18:3

W hy is it that few men attend prayer meetings? I noticed this
at my church and started to wonder about it. Then I realized, "It
is because women are incubators. If they are presented with an
idea, a need, or a problem, they will take it to heart and will work
through it until they arrive at a solution."

Just as a womb nourishes a fetus during development and an
incubator protects premature or sick babies, a woman has a nurturing instinct that can be a powerful source of encouragement
in the lives of others. If a man wants something prayed about, he
should tell a woman. She'll take the circumstance into her spiritual womb, where she meets with God in her inner being, incubate
it for months, if necessary, and bring forth a solution. She won't
give up until she receives an answer from God.

Jesus didn't say that it was a man who kept knocking at the
judge's door in order to obtain justice. (See Luke 18:2–8.) It wasn't
a man who persisted with the Lord Jesus for a healing for her
daughter, saying, *"Even the dogs eat the crumbs that fall from their
master's table"* (Matthew 15:27). Do you know to whom God first
gave the resurrection message? Women. It was the women who
first saw the resurrected Christ and went to tell the men. Why?
Because the men had locked themselves in their room! (See John
20:19.) Note also that Jesus gave the woman at the well a message, and she turned it into an entire evangelistic team. (See John

4:4–30.) Women are spiritual incubators who birth spiritual results in God.

～

*Thought*: A woman won't give up in prayer until she receives an answer from God.

*Readings*: 1 Samuel 1:1–20; Luke 18:1–8

# ANCHORED ON THE ROCK

*"We have this hope as an anchor for the soul, firm and secure. It enters the inner sanctuary behind the curtain, where our forerunner, Jesus, has entered on our behalf. He has become a high priest forever, in the order of Melchizedek."*

—Hebrews 6:19–20

The word *Bahamas* means "shallow waters," but there's a place where the sea drops off about six thousand feet, which is called the tongue of the ocean. Once my associates and I had gone spear fishing, and we were diving at a reef right next to the tongue. As long as our boat stayed in the shallow area, the anchor held because it could reach rock at the bottom. But then the anchor got into some sand, and the current from the tongue of the ocean started dragging the boat.

When the boat drifted over the tongue, the anchor had nothing to hold on to; it was thousands of feet above the bottom of the ocean. When we noticed what was happening, we were on the reef yelling for the captain to come, and he was trying to start the engine, but the engine wouldn't start! He was drifting over the depths of the ocean.

That was a moment I'll never forget. We were about fifty feet from the tongue where there were massive sharks. We were stranded on the reef, there was a strong current that could pull us toward the tongue, and our only refuge was that boat. At that point, the boat's anchor was useless as our security because it had nothing to hold on to. After being out all night in the darkness, we were finally rescued. Our families had contacted the equivalent of the Coast Guard in the Bahamas, and a ship came and found us.

You are not strong enough to keep your family's "boat" secure if you as the anchor have nothing solid to hold on to. If you can't hold steady and you get "lost at sea," what will they do? Make sure you are holding *firm and secure* to Jesus Christ. (See Hebrews 6:19.)

*Thought*: As heavy as an anchor is, it needs to rest on something heavier to enable it to hold steady.

*Readings*: Psalm 18:30–32; 1 Peter 2:4–6

# PARENTS AND PURPOSE

*"Fathers, do not exasperate your children; instead, bring them up in the training and instruction of the Lord."*

—Ephesians 6:4

Did Jesus have an adolescent problem? The answer is, very simply, no. Why? One reason is that His purpose was reinforced by His earthly father and mother from birth. Somehow I believe that God would love for all parents to know Him so well that they would have an idea of the life purpose of their children.

The angel Gabriel said to Mary, *"You will conceive and give birth to a son, and you are to call him Jesus. He will be great and will be called the Son of the Most High"* (Luke 1:31–32). An angel of the Lord told Joseph, *"You are to give him the name Jesus, because he will save his people from their sins"* (Matthew 1:21). When Jesus was born, Mary and Joseph could talk to Him about His purpose. Even though, at the time, they didn't fully understand the implications of His name, they could tell Him, "You're going to be a Savior." The Hebrew meaning of the name *Jesus* is "Jehovah-saved," or "the Lord is salvation." In essence, Jesus's name means "Savior."

I can't emphasize strongly enough that knowing your purpose is crucial for your life's course. Every young person comes to a time when he or she leaves childhood and enters adulthood. This is the time when they are trying to discover who they are and why they are. This is also often the time when we lose them or gain them— lose them to a destructive lifestyle and a wasted life or gain them for a positive, fulfilling future. Purpose, therefore, is a key to a young person's effectiveness and happiness in life.

Proverbs 19:18 says, *"Discipline your children, for in that there is hope; do not be a willing party to their death."* This is serious business. The verse is saying, "Discipline and train a child now because there is hope in that discipline, hope in that training." You are giving hope to your child when you discipline and correct him because *you are giving him a value system for his entire life!*

The above verse makes the strong statement that if you don't do this, you may be a party to your child's death. Proverbs 29:15 says, *"A child left undisciplined disgraces its mother."* Check out the children in the reform schools. Check out the inmates in the prisons. Look at the people living on the streets. Observe the young people who have little sense of direction or morality. Many of them were left to themselves as children, with no one to teach them character and values.

*Thought*: When you discipline and correct your child you are giving him a value system for his entire life.

*Readings*: Proverbs 1:1–9; Luke 2

# TEACH YOUR CHILDREN AND GRANDCHILDREN

*"Teach them to your children and to their children after them."*                    —Deuteronomy 4:9

In Deuteronomy, Moses gave instructions from God to the heads of households about teaching their families God's ways:

> *Be careful, and watch yourselves closely so that you do not forget the things your eyes have seen or let them fade from your heart as long as you live. Teach them to your children and to their children after them.* (Deuteronomy 4:9)

God is very concerned that parents teach their children about Him. He isn't saying here to send your children to church, Sunday school, or vacation Bible club. He's saying to teach them yourself. These other activities are good, but if what they teach is not reinforced in the home, children can get the impression their parents don't think the Bible is important. Parents don't realize the negative impact this attitude can have on their families.

*"...and to their children after them."* I want to say a word here to grandparents. When your daughter or son sends that little boy or girl to you, what does the child go back home with? Some kids learn things from their grandparents that are disgraceful. Parents find their little children coming back home cursing or telling foul stories, and they wonder where they are hearing them. They're getting them from Grandpa and Grandma! Your children's children should get the Word from you. Timothy received a strong spiritual heritage from both his mother and his grandmother. Paul wrote, *"I am reminded of your sincere faith, which first lived in your*

*grandmother Lois and in your mother Eunice and, I am persuaded, now lives in you also*" (2 Timothy 1:5).

When your children send their kids to you, those kids should go back home knowing more about God.

∽

*Thought*: God is very concerned that parents teach their children about Him.

*Readings*: Proverbs 20:15; Ephesians 4:29

# FORTIFY YOUR CHILDREN
# THROUGH THE WORD

*"These commandments that I give you today are to be upon your hearts. Impress them on your children. Talk about them when you sit at home and when you walk along the road, when you lie down and when you get up. Tie them as symbols on your hands and bind them on your foreheads. Write them on the doorframes of your houses and on your gates."*

—Deuteronomy 6:6–9

Reflecting on the above Scripture passage, let's look at four specific ways in which God told Moses that parents are to talk to their children about His commandments.

*"Talk about them when you sit at home."* What do your children hear in your house? What do they hear when you sit down to eat? Some scandal reported in the newspaper? The latest movie? What do you discuss? Do you talk about the goodness of the Lord? When you sit around your house during your leisure time, what do you do? Do you spend time teaching your children the Word? Do you have family devotions?

*"Talk about them...when you walk along the road."* What do you talk about when you drive your children to school or go on trips? Do you yell at other drivers or listen to less-than-edifying radio shows? What example do you set for your children when you're out in public? Do you talk about others behind their backs? Or do you live out God's Word in a natural, everyday way?

*"Talk about them...when you lie down"* (Deuteronomy 6:7). Before you say good night to your children or tuck them into bed, what words do you leave them with? The assurance of God's

presence and peace during the night? An encouraging psalm? Or do you wave them off to bed while you finish working on something?

In fact, what do you think about before you drift off to sleep? Do you know that the last thing you think about at night is usually the first thing you think about when you wake up? Sometimes you dream about it. It amazes me that people deliberately think about the worst things. You may be reading the worst kind of books before you go to bed. Then you wonder why your spirit is disturbed.

*"Talk about them…when you get up."* When you wake up in the morning, you will more likely think about the Word of God if you have meditated on it before going to bed. And you will start ministering as you talk about it with your family.

How do you usually greet your children in the morning? With a quiet reminder of God's love and strength for the day? With what spiritual armor do you send them off to school? It's a difficult world for children to grow up in today, and they need God's Word to fortify them for daily living.

⌒

*Thought*: Children need the Word of God to fortify them for daily living.

*Readings*: Deuteronomy 6; James 1:22–25

# CONDITION YOUR CHILDREN

*"Train a child in the way he should go, and when he is old he will not turn from it."*  —Proverbs 22:6 (NIV84)

If you train your children, they will grow up to know God's ways and to have peace in their hearts. The things children learn from their parents never leave them. I still retain what my father and mother taught me. The same temptations that come to any young man came to me. What kept me on an even keel were the values and morals that were instilled in me. There were situations where, if it wasn't for the training of my parents, I would have gone under. What kept me safe was the character I learned from their teaching and correction. I love my parents because they disciplined me.

My parents had a wonderful way of sitting me down and saying, "Now, here is why we disciplined you." They didn't just punish me; they corrected me. They said, "If you keep this up, this will happen," and "If you keep this kind of company, this will be the result." Disciplining your children will be painful for both you and your children at times, but the results will be positive and healthy.

My heart goes out to single parents who have to fill the roles of both father and mother. I strongly want to encourage you not to let your children train you. Don't allow them to reverse the roles of parent and child. You may not know everything in life, but you know more than they do! And that's enough for you to be in charge. I don't care how old they are, when you're paying the mortgage, when you're providing for them, you make the rules. If they disobey the rules, you have to make sure they experience the consequences.

*"Train a child in the way he should go..."* (Proverbs 22:6). The word for *"train"* in this verse is the same word that is used for conditioning. The Bible is saying, "Condition your child in the way he should go." Why? He can't condition himself. He was born with a rebellious spirit. You don't have to teach your children to swear, lie, steal, commit adultery, or have bitterness and hatred. It's already in them. If you don't condition them, they will naturally become wayward. You have to train them. If you seek and trust Him, the Lord will provide everything you need to help you fulfill this role, whether you are in a two-parent family or are a single parent. *"A father to the fatherless, a defender of widows, is God in his holy dwelling"* (Psalm 68:5).

⌒

*Thought*: Disciplining your children will be painful for both you and your children at times, but the results will be positive and healthy.

*Readings*: Proverbs 29:17; Ephesians 6:1–4

# ENCOURAGE AND COMFORT
# YOUR CHILDREN

*"For you know that we dealt with each of you as a father deals with his own children, encouraging, comforting and urging [or warning] you to live lives worthy of God, who calls you into his kingdom and glory."* —1 Thessalonians 2:11–12

Children need encouragement. Some children never hear an encouraging word from their parents. Do you hear how some parents talk to their children? They act as if the children can't do anything right. They don't remember what it is like to be a child, and they expect their children to have adult skills. A ten-year-old boy is washing the dishes. His father comes in and says, "Can't you clean dishes better than this?" The little guy is at least trying. So encourage him. Maybe he leaves a little soap on the stove or counter. Don't look at what he left; look at what he cleaned up. Encourage him.

Maybe your child can't read quite as fast as you did when you were her age. Don't criticize her. Encourage her. Some children are really trying. Sometimes a child will try to help out with the chores and will unintentionally break something. His mother will run into the room and yell, "What are you doing?" He gets a lecture. So he goes to his room with a broken heart, a depressed spirit, and a hurt ego. He thinks, *I'm not going to help ever again!* Some parents don't see their child's intention. They see only their own anger and frustration. So, correct and instruct your children with patience, and encourage their efforts.

Children also need comforting. You encourage them when they're doing something positive, and when you want them to improve in something. But there will be times when they become discouraged, hurt, confused, or disillusioned. That is when they need comfort.

How can you comfort your children? By letting them know they are loved, even when they make mistakes or don't live up to your expectations. By listening to their struggles and problems with kindness and understanding. By giving them warm embraces and loving words when they are sad. By remembering the times God has comforted you in your distress and giving that same comfort to them.

To be a comforter, you have to be accessible to your children. You have to know what's going on in their lives so you can know when they're experiencing struggles and loneliness. Children will be comforted to know you're available to them and that you make it a point to spend time with them. Your comfort will also help them to know that their heavenly Father is a Comforter, just as He is described in His Word: *"the Father of compassion and the God of all comfort, who comforts us in all our troubles"* (2 Corinthians 1:3–4).

⌒

*Thought*: Comforting your children will help them to know that their heavenly Father is a Comforter.

*Readings*: Job 16:1–5; 2 Corinthians 1:3–6

# WARN YOUR CHILDREN

*"[Christ] is the one we proclaim, admonishing and teaching everyone with all wisdom, so that we may present everyone fully mature in Christ."* —Colossians 1:28

The Bible points out that conscientious parents warn their children *"to live lives worthy of God"* (1 Thessalonians 2:12). It is the parents' responsibility to warn their children of the consequences of rejecting God. "Son, there is an eternal hell. I warn you, whatever you sow on earth, you're going to reap in eternity." "Daughter, I warn you that whatever you become involved in can follow you in your memory forever." These are examples of spiritual warning.

When humanity rejected God, He gave them what they wanted. He gave them over to their passions. That's not as simple as it might sound. If God had just given us over to what we wanted, the implication might have been that we could succeed in spite of Him. But when God gave us over, He also allowed us to experience the inevitable results of our actions. God didn't just say, "Okay, go, carry on." He said, "If you carry on, you're going to end up depraved, because that isn't the way I made you." (See Romans 1:28.)

Parents are to urge or warn their children to live righteously. Yet how many parents confuse warning with threatening? "I'm going to kill you if you don't stop that!" Some parents don't have any kind of tact because they don't know any better. A child interprets a warning as love but sees a threat as hate.

Many parents warn their children, but their children don't listen to them because they aren't setting a godly example. Are you setting a good example for your children by walking in God's ways? What are they observing about the way you live your life and the consequences of your actions? If you are walking in God's ways when you warn your children, they will come to respect the God of their parents. They will say, "If I obey my parents, then I'm obeying my God. I know that my parents know what is best because I see God working in their lives. I'll obey my parents because I want God to work in my life, too."

Warn your children. It's your responsibility.

Thought: Are you setting a good example for your children by walking in God's ways?

Readings: Psalm 19:8–13; Titus 2:1–8

# PERFECTLY COMPLEMENTARY DESIGNS

*"The eye cannot say to the hand, 'I don't need you!' And the
head cannot say to the feet, 'I don't need you!'"*
—1 Corinthians 12:21

God created men and women with perfectly complementary
designs. The male is perfect for the female, and the female is perfect for the male. It is when men and women expect each other
to think, react, and behave in the same ways—that is, when they
don't know or appreciate their God-given differences—that they
experience conflict. Yet when they understand and value each other's purposes, they can have rewarding relationships, and they can
blend their unique designs harmoniously for God's glory.

Many husbands and wives don't realize that the needs of their
spouses are different from their own. There is a principle that
"purpose determines nature, and nature determines needs." If a
woman wants to help a man fulfill his purpose, she must learn his
nature, how he functions, and what his needs are. She can't give
him what she needs, because his needs are often different from
hers. The reverse is also true. A man must learn a woman's needs
and seek to meet them.

God has given strengths to the female that the male does not
possess, and vice versa. Until they recognize the natures God has
placed within each of them, they will be weak in certain areas,
because each was designed to supply what the other lacks. Males
and females have different strengths, and neither can fully function without the other.

The designs of males and females govern the needs of each that must be met for them to be fulfilled, contented, and living in God's creation purposes. The problem is that many people are not fully aware of their own needs, let alone the needs of others. Even when people are aware of their needs, they often live in frustration because their needs are not being met. They end up demanding that another person satisfy them or they suffer in silence, never expecting to live a completely fulfilled life.

In the next few devotionals, we will explore the paramount needs of the female and the male that contribute to a fulfilling relationship. Please keep in mind that the needs that are listed as female needs and the needs that are listed as male needs are also the needs of both. However, they will be discussed in the context of the *primary* needs of each.

As we come to understand one another's needs and work to fulfill them, our hearts and minds will be renewed and more of God's creation purposes will be restored to our lives. In this endeavor, Jesus's great principle, *"It is more blessed to give than to receive"* (Acts 20:35), is vital. As you give, meeting the needs of others, you will be blessed, and many of your own needs will be met in return.

⌒

*Thought*: When men and women understand and value each other's purposes, they can have rewarding relationships.

*Readings*: Genesis 2:23; 1 Corinthians 12:12–26

# NEED FOR LOVE/RESPECT

*"Each one of you [husbands] also must love his wife as he loves himself, and the wife must respect her husband."*
—Ephesians 5:33

In the above verse, the apostle Paul emphasized the primary needs of men and women, which we began to look at in earlier devotionals. Because she was created for the purpose of receiving love, a woman doesn't just desire love; she truly requires it. A woman wants to feel that she is important and special to her husband. When a man spends time with a woman, it makes her feel cherished because she knows she comes first in his life. She feels cared for when he goes out of his way to make sure she has everything she needs.

As much as a woman needs to feel that she is loved, a man needs to know that he is respected. Being respected is at the core of his self-esteem, and it affects every other area of his life. It is part of his nature as leader, protector, and provider. A wife can meet her husband's need for admiration and respect by understanding his value and achievements more than anyone else. She needs to remind him of his capabilities and help him to maintain his self-confidence. She should be proud of her husband, not out of duty, but as an expression of sincere admiration for the man with whom she has chosen to share her life.

We should remember that a single man needs respect as much as a married man does. He needs the respect and affirmation of women because he is designed to need it. The women in a single man's life can meet his need by recognizing his value and accomplishments as a man and by encouraging him in his talents and lifework.

Because the female's primary need is for love, she often thinks that the male's primary need is for love, also. He needs love, but his need for respect is even greater. If a female expresses love to a male, without fulfilling his need for respect, he might not respond in the way she expects him to. He might remain somewhat distant. For example, a woman may wonder why her husband doesn't seem satisfied in the relationship when she has been lovingly trying to help him by keeping the household running smoothly and providing for his material needs. A woman might even write her husband love notes and give him lots of affection but notice that he still doesn't seem happy. She wonders, *What else can I do for this man?*

Yet a male feels about those things in the same way that a female feels about the male's provision of a house. He is grateful that his material and emotional needs are being taken care of, and he appreciates his wife's efforts. However, these things don't address his primary need. A husband is to love and cherish his wife. A wife is to respect and honor her husband. In this way, there will be a constant meeting of the other's primary needs.

⌒

*Thought*: Build up your spouse by meeting his or her primary need.

*Readings*: Proverbs 31:23; 1 Peter 1:22

# SUPPORTING, NOT COMPARING

*"Her husband has full confidence in her and lacks nothing of value. She brings him good, not harm, all the days of her life."* —Proverbs 31:11–12

The woman is meant to bless, support, and honor the man, and the man is meant to be a head, a covering, and a protection for her. In this way, they are helping each other to be all they were created to be. Yet these purposes break down when the man and the woman don't know or address each other's needs.

A woman who is struggling with her husband's lack of vision or spiritual immaturity may begin to compare him with other Christian men. The worst thing a woman can do is to compare her husband with another man. Ladies, please don't tell your husbands, "Why can't you be like our pastor?" or "Why aren't you like so-and-so?" That's the most dangerous—and ridiculous—thing a woman can say to a man. Every man is his own being and has his own image of himself. Again, you need to support him, even if he is not perfect; you need to be an encouragement to him in his life.

For example, a man always wants to feel as if he is a leader. Try to make your husband feel that he has contributed significantly to your family's success. When you make a man feel that he is important to what has been accomplished—that he is the one responsible for, or that his input was necessary for, the success of something—then you will have somebody who serves you, because a man feeds on respect. However, if you make him feel unimportant, you will run into trouble. "Well, I don't need you anyway; I've already been doing this for ten years without you." When you communicate that kind of idea to a man, he will back further and further away from you.

~~~

*Thought*: The worst thing a woman can do is to compare her husband to another man.

*Readings*: Proverbs 25:24; Philippians 4:4–5

# WHAT DO I DO IN THE MEANTIME?

*"Be patient, bearing with one another in love."*
—Ephesians 4:2

One of the problems a woman may face is that her husband doesn't know he's supposed to love her in the ways we've been talking about. Even though a woman might be honoring and esteeming her husband, he might not be showing her love because he really doesn't yet know how. This is a very real problem for many wives, who may wonder, *What do I do in the meantime?* While men and women need to understand and meet each other's needs, if the woman understands the needs of both men and women but her spouse doesn't, it is important that she have patience. She needs to respond to her husband according to what he does know.

If I know that a person is ignorant, I can't be angry at them. Jesus is the highest model of this for us. He said, *"Father, forgive them, for they do not know what they are doing"* (Luke 23:34). The difficulty comes when you know that a person is aware of what he's supposed to be doing but still doesn't do it. In this case, some kind of reproof is necessary. Depending on the situation, a woman might appeal directly to her husband; or she might appeal to the pastor, a trusted Christian friend, or even a family member to speak to her husband for her. Yet her best appeal is to pray for her husband and allow the Lord to change him.

You can reprove a person who has knowledge, but you need to overlook the faults of a person who is ignorant. This will keep bitterness from taking over your heart. Avoid blaming the other person, live responsibly before God, and make sure you carry out your own responsibilities to your spouse. *"That they may be won over without words by the behavior of their wives"* (1 Peter 3:1).

~

*Thought*: Trust God to teach your partner how to meet your needs.

*Readings*: Psalm 28:7; Philippians 4:6–7

# NEED FOR CONVERSATION/RECREATION

*"The pleasantness of a friend springs from their heartfelt advice."* —Proverbs 27:9

A woman has a need for conversation. Yet, because males have a leadership mind-set, sometimes their conversations with their wives amount to instructions rather than a give-and-take dialogue. A woman desires to have a man talk *with* her, not *at* her.

Some men don't realize that a woman has a need to express herself and therefore has much within her that she wants to share. A man can fulfill a woman's need for intimate conversation by continually making a point to communicate with her. To truly meet her need, he should talk with her at the *feeling* level and not just the knowledge and information level. She needs him to listen to her attitudes about the events of her day with sensitivity, interest, and concern, resisting the impulse to offer quick solutions. Instead, he should offer his full attention and understanding. All of his conversations with her should convey a desire to understand her, not to change her.

A man's competitive nature leads to his need for recreational companionship, his need to be involved in challenging activities. Although he likes to win, he also desires to share these experiences with others. Nothing blesses a man more than when a woman is involved in his favorite recreation. If a wife participates in what her husband enjoys doing and lets him tell her all about it, she can strengthen her relationship with him. He will feel good that she is involved in his interests.

I've heard women say things like this about their husbands: "That old fool; he's always over at the ball field playing softball. I wish he would stop that and come home and be a husband." This attitude won't help the situation. He has a need that is being met out there on the ball field. Why would a man spend hours on something unless he has a need that is being fulfilled through it? Instead of fighting against what brings fulfillment to the man, the woman should find out why it is important to him. Then, if possible, she should participate in it so that they can experience it together, thus building understanding, companionship, and intimacy in their relationship.

⁓

*Thought*: A male needs to share his interests, and a female needs conversation: these related needs can be a wonderful bridge of communication between men and women.

*Readings*: Genesis 2:18; John 4:4–39

# NEED FOR AFFECTION/SEX

*"My beloved is mine and I am his."* —Song of Songs 2:16

A woman needs affection. She doesn't just want affection—she needs it! Yet while one of her primary needs is affection, one of the male's primary needs is sex. If these two interrelated needs are not lovingly understood and balanced, they can cause some of the worst conflicts in a marriage.

It is important for a woman to be sensitive to her husband's need for sex. Sometimes, a woman sees a man's sexual energy as animalistic and thoughtless. If his approach is too abrupt or too aggressive, she may tell him to leave her alone. There are also times when she is not ready for sexual relations because of her cycle, so she will put him off. In these situations, the man may interpret her refusals as disinterest or disrespect, instead of recognizing the underlying reasons behind them.

What women and men need to understand is that *affection creates the environment for sexual union* in marriage, while *sex is the event.* Most men don't realize this, and so they immediately go after the event. They don't know what it means to create an environment of affection. They focus only on their need. Women need affection to precede sexual intimacy.

The man is the provider of the seed, and therefore his natural inclination is to provide this source. This is one of the reasons why he concentrates on the event of sex. The woman, on the other hand, is the one who gestates the new life. Her role is to provide a warm and secure environment in which the life can grow and develop. As an incubator, the woman's natural focus is on the sensory, intuitive, and emotional realms of life, and this is why she has a corresponding need for affection. She needs an environment of affection in order to feel loved and fulfilled.

The problem is that most males are not naturally affectionate. Many men simply do not understand how to give affection to their wives. If a husband is not sure how to be affectionate, he should sit down with his wife and ask her—gently and sincerely.

Giving affection to a woman means appealing to that which makes her an emotional being. Sometimes a woman just wants her husband to sit with her, hold her hand, and talk with her. Her need can also be met by plenty of hugs and kisses; a steady flow of words, cards, and flowers; common courtesies; and meaningful gifts that show that the man is thinking of her—that he esteems her and values her presence in his life.

The Bible says that husbands and wives are to fulfill one another's sexual needs. (See 1 Corinthians 7:3–5.) It also says that a husband is to be sensitive to his wife's overall needs, treating her with kindness and respect. Men and women must balance having their own needs fulfilled with showing consideration for one another.

⌒

*Thought*: Affection creates the environment for sexual union in marriage, while sex is the event.

*Readings*: Genesis 24; 1 Corinthians 7:3–5

# SEX IS GOD'S IDEA

*"God saw all that he had made, and it was very good."*
—Genesis 1:31

How do we know that sex is a good thing? God created man and woman and their sexual nature. Therefore, He said that sex is *"very good."*

Unfortunately, sexuality is often extremely misunderstood—not only in the secular world, but also in the church. I am deeply concerned about the damage this lack of understanding about sex has done—and is doing—to people's lives. It has led to confusion and broken relationships between women and men. It has prevented males from living up to their full potential as men and husbands. It has destroyed marriages—and lives. My prayer is that women and men will find wholeness in God as they understand His purpose and plan for human sexuality.

God is not negative about sex. He *created* it. (See Genesis 1:28.) Sex is God's idea, not man's idea. It is such a beautiful expression of love and giving that only God could have thought of it. Men and women were designed as sexual beings. Every baby is born as a sexual creature with the potential to have a sexual relationship as an adult. God is negative only about the *misuse* of sex because it harms the people He created to have a fulfilling relationship with the opposite sex. We must realize that the Bible itself is very open about the subject of sexuality. The main theme of the book of Song of Songs is sexual love. It is the story of a young bridegroom and his bride and their love and desire for one another.

Why did God create sex? The primary reason is that unity is a central aspect of God's nature and purposes. In the Bible, the sexual union of marriage is used as a metaphor to describe the intimacy between Christ and the church. The picture of Christ as the Bridegroom and the church as the bride gives us an idea of the preciousness with which God views sex. He views it as a symbol of His oneness with His beloved humanity, who have been created in His image and redeemed through His love.

⌒

*Thought*: God is negative only about the *misuse* of sex because it harms the people He created to have a fulfilling relationship with the opposite sex.

*Readings*: Isaiah 62:4–5; Revelation 19:6–9

# IGNORANCE ABOUT SEXUALITY

*"Do not conform to the pattern of this world, but be transformed by the renewing of your mind."*     —Romans 12:2

Some of you are suffering right now from the consequences of uninformed or unwise sexual activity. How a person first learned about sex determines, to a great degree, how he engages in it.

How did you first learn about sexuality? When I've asked men in my seminars how they were introduced to the concept of sex, they've listed various sources, such as friends or peers, movies and television, biology books, pornographic magazines or videos, and sexual experimentation during youth. When we receive our information about sex from one or more of these sources and then pass along this information to others, we perpetuate cultural ignorance about sexuality. This is what has been happening in many of our societies. A lot of what we have learned about sex has been acquired in an unwholesome context, and it is filled with misinformation. Men and women lack positive, informed teaching on the subject of sexuality.

Much of the blame for this lack of teaching falls on the church and the home. In general, the message we've heard from our churches and families is that sex is unholy or dirty and should not be discussed. Young people get the idea that parents and children aren't supposed to talk about sex, because their own parents don't discuss it with them. They are prevented from expressing their sexual questions in the context of a loving home or church community, so they seek information from other sources. When we neglect to teach our children God's truth about sex, then we abandon them to the culture for their information.

No one has a right to shape your child's concept and attitudes about sex, except you. Make sure that a questionable sex education class or *Playboy* magazine isn't your child's teacher. Train your child in the way he or she should go. Then, when a friend or teacher starts to say something erroneous about sex, your child can dismiss it with the knowledge, "That isn't what my parents told me. I know that isn't the truth."

*Thought:* When we neglect to teach our children God's truth about sex, then we abandon them to the culture for their information.

*Readings:* Proverbs 5:15–23; Hebrews 13:4

# A PROTECTIVE BOUNDARY

*"A man leaves his father and mother and is united to his wife, and they become one flesh."* —Genesis 2:24

The boundary God has given us to enjoy sex safely is the marriage covenant. Sex must be engaged in only in the context of marriage—a solemn, lifelong commitment between two people before God.

The Scripture says that a man is to *"bring happiness to the wife he has married"* (Deuteronomy 24:5). It doesn't say to move in with somebody for a year and try things out. There are no provisionary covenants. Solomon said, *"May you rejoice in the wife of your youth.... May her breasts satisfy you always, may you ever be intoxicated by her love"* (Proverbs 5:18–19). This passage is a reference to sex. Enjoy *"the wife of your youth"*—not someone else. There is a vacuum in the male that needs to be filled by the female. And God says, "Make sure your wife is the one who fills that vacuum."

The Scripture says, *"That is why a man leaves his father and mother and is united to his wife, and they become one flesh"* (Genesis 2:24). *"That is why."* For what reason should a man leave? To be *"united."* To whom? *"To his wife."* The minute that law is violated, we begin to reap the repercussions. Verse 24 says, *"And they become one flesh."* The boundary that God has established for the one-flesh experience is the husband and wife relationship.

*"All other sins a person commits are outside the body, but whoever sins sexually, sins against their own body"* (1 Corinthians 6:18). Some people can't understand why couples who sleep together and then break off their relationship have trouble going their separate ways.

It is because the separation causes real trauma in their souls. This is a serious matter. That's why relationships outside God's plan can be so dangerous.

Your body belongs to God twice. He didn't just create you; He also redeemed you, and the price was high—the life of His Son Jesus. How can you honor God with your body? First, by waiting until you're married to engage in sex; second, by having sex only with your spouse. You are God's temple. You lift up your hands to worship God; you can use those same hands to caress your spouse. Both acts are holy in His sight.

⌒

*Thought:* The primary boundary God has given us to enjoy sex safely is the marriage covenant.

*Readings:* Malachi 2:13–16; 1 Corinthians 6:12–20

# DIFFERENCES IN COMMUNICATION STYLES

*"We have different gifts, according to the grace given to each of us."* —Romans 12:6

Paul was writing about spiritual gifts in the above verse, but the same idea applies to the different communication styles women and men display. In His purpose and grace, God made women and men very different from each other in the way they think, act, and respond. These differences were designed to be complementary and not divisive.

In upcoming devotionals, we will be discussing the basic natures and tendencies of females and males in communication. Of course, there will always be exceptions, for every person is unique. Yet within the variations, the general tendencies usually hold true.

Adam and Eve originally lived in harmony with God, and so they were able to live in harmony with one another. They knew how to draw on each other's strengths in communication for the betterment of them both. However, when humanity turned away from God's purposes and broke relationship with Him, the lines of communication between males and females were cut or, at least, badly frayed. Thus, the differences that were originally designed for mutual support now often lead to misunderstandings and conflicts in marriage and in other relationships between women and men.

The chances are very good that you have experienced some of these misunderstanding and conflicts firsthand! Handling differences of opinion and avoiding discord are universal problems in relationships. How can you to live harmoniously with a spouse whom you love but who processes information and responds in a manner that is different from the way that you do? Women and men must be brought into the complementary balance that was God's original purpose for them. This balance will be achieved when we understand the strengths of each communication style and learn to communicate with each other according to the style that the other party can receive and understand.

With this knowledge—and some patience and forgiveness—women and men who are seeking God's redemptive purposes for their lives can communicate effectively and happily with one another. When they are considerate of each another, they have the basis on which they can develop the mutual love and respect that is crucial to lasting relationships.

⌇

*Thought*: God made women and men very different from each other in the way they think, act, and respond.

*Readings*: Psalm 37:37; Romans 12:3–8

# "EMOTIONAL FEELER" AND
# "LOGICAL THINKER"

*"How many are your works, L*ORD*! In wisdom you made them all."* —Psalm 104:24

God made the woman primarily as an "emotional feeler" and the man chiefly as a "logical thinker." This does not mean that women do not use logic or that men do not have emotions. They each just have a specific way of looking at the world. When I state that a woman is an emotional feeler, I am referring to the way in which she processes the verbal and nonverbal communication she receives from the world around her. Because the woman is an incubator, she not only receives thoughts and ideas into her being, but also transforms them as she processes them in her emotional, mental, and spiritual wombs. Her communication style reflects this process. When a woman receives information, she assesses it both mentally and emotionally *at the same time.* This is what makes her distinct from the male, who generally uses these functions separately.

God's creation is remarkable. He actually designed the brains of females and males to be different. The neural pathways between the left and right hemispheres of a woman's brain (both the logical and the emotional sides) are intact. This explains what often puzzles many men: women's ability to do multiple tasks at the same time rather than having to focus on just one. The woman's brain allows her to process facts and feelings almost simultaneously. Her emotions are with her all the time she is thinking, and this influences her perspective on the world around her as well as what is communicated to her.

There are fewer nerves connecting the two hemispheres of the male's brain, so the logical and emotional sides are not as closely connected. Because of this, a man basically needs to "shift gears" to move from his dominant logical side to his emotional side. This is why men, in general, think in terms of facts and in a linear fashion. They think like a straight line—the shortest distance between two points—which gives them the ability to see the goal (the vision) and to focus their energies on reaching it in the most straightforward and direct way.

Women, on the other hand, tend to think more like a grid than a straight line. A woman's brain is designed to pick up many details that men don't "see"—things that go beyond the mere facts, such as the personalities, motivations, and feelings of both herself and others. She can perceive, evaluate, and see relationships between things all at the same time, like x, y, and z coordinates on a grid track multiple factors at the same time.

No one person, and no one gender, can look at the world with complete perspective. Therefore, God has designed things so that when the female and the male work together in unity, they can help one another to see a more balanced picture of life. They weren't meant to understand the world and fulfill their dominion mandate in isolation from one another. For this reason, they have built-in ways of seeing the world that are of benefit to each other.

⌒

*Thought*: No one person, and no one gender, can look at the world with complete perspective.

*Readings*: Psalm 139:1–3; Philippians 4:8

# A BEAUTIFUL COMPLEMENT

*"Two are better than one, because they have a good return for their labor: if either of them falls down, one can help the other up."* —Ecclesiastes 4:9–10

The distinct differences between women and men are meant to be a help to them—not a hindrance or a source of pain. One way of thinking and communicating is not better than the other way, and the inherent differences between the two are not a result of the fall of humanity. The way women and men are designed is for their good. They just need to exercise patience and understanding and to value the other's contribution.

The female's emotional feeling will balance the male's logical thinking. Many women don't understand how important they are to the men in their lives. The female was created to help the male in that whatever the man lacks, the woman possesses. The reverse is also true. This principle is based on God's purpose.

If women and men are not careful, they will come to conclusions about each other's motivations without knowing what the woman is really thinking or the man is really feeling. This has caused many people to think that their marriages or relationships aren't working. After a while, they say, "Forget this," and they walk away. Later on, they meet somebody else and get married, hoping things will be different this time. However, they encounter the same problems that they did in their previous relationships. They think the problem is with the other person, when the problem is often with the inability of both parties to communicate well. This cycle will continue until they learn to understand and work through the differences between women and men, why each is unique, and how God has made them to complement one another beautifully.

⌒

*Thought*: The next time you are tempted to label a male as "unfeeling," stop and appreciate their unique outlook, which brings balance and perspective to your life.

*Readings*: Ecclesiastes 4:9–12; Ephesians 4:3

# FEELING, THINKING, AND SELF-EXPRESSION

*"Let us therefore make every effort to do what leads to peace and to mutual edification."* —Romans 14:19

Communication between women and men comes down to *feeling, thinking,* and *self-expression.* Women and men both feel. Women and men both think. It is their manner of looking at the world and their self-expression that makes the difference. A woman's first reaction will generally be an emotional one, followed by a thinking one. A man's first reaction will be a thinking one, but he will also feel.

Women often have been written off as foolish and inferior by men because they are expressive and show their emotions. A woman does not need to apologize for her emotions. God made her to feel. Males have assumed that their approach is better than the females' approach rather than complementary to it. They haven't known or understood how and why the woman was created to be an emotional feeler.

The woman can help the man see aspects of life that, if overlooked or ignored, can become detours or potholes preventing him from reaching his goal or from reaching it as quickly as he might have. Her peripheral vision keeps him from being blindsided as he single-mindedly pursues his goals and objectives. On the other hand, the man's linear thinking helps the woman not to become so enmeshed in the many layers of her multidimensional thinking that she loses sight of the goal and never reaches it.

Let's look at a situation highlighting these different perspectives. A married couple plans a romantic evening together. The wife looks forward to an evening with her husband. She prepares the food, sets the table, arranges the flowers, and then meets him at the door when he comes home. Her husband walks in, says hello, then strides right past her without noticing that she has dressed up. He goes into the living room and says, "I'm going to have dinner in front of the TV while I watch the news." His mind is still in work mode, intent on finding out any information that may affect his work and thus his ability to provide. Because his wife doesn't understand this, she is deeply hurt at his behavior; her first reaction is to feel that he is ungrateful and inconsiderate. She approaches him angrily. Surprised, he asks, "What's the matter with you?"

At this point, she sees nothing complementary in the way he is designed! When we don't understand purpose, we begin to misinterpret motives. It is this suspicion that creates conflict. This is why understanding purpose and design is so important. Both the woman's reaction and the man's reaction are related to the way they are made. She took his apparent indifference personally, while his mind was so preoccupied with what he was thinking that he did not notice what his wife was feeling.

Women and men need each other in order to chart the best course in life—one that enables them to reach their common goal but also experience their journey in the fullest, wisest, and most rewarding way possible.

⌒

*Thought*: Women and men need each other to chart the best course in life.

*Readings*: Proverbs 10:11–12; 1 Peter 4:8

# ARE WE HEARING THE SAME THING?

*"I love the LORD, because He has heard my voice and my supplications. Because He has inclined His ear to me, therefore I will call upon Him as long as I live."*

—Psalm 116:1–2 (NKJV)

What a woman hears, she receives as an emotional experience; what a man hears, he generally receives merely as information. They have two entirely different ways of processing language that is spoken to them.

The woman receives language in an emotional way because she is designed to absorb the world around her and to personalize it. She is designed to take in everything and incubate it. A man doesn't usually have an emotional experience with what he hears. This is why it is very important for a male to understand a female. Before a man speaks to a woman, he needs to think about what he is about to say and how he is about to say it. Because a woman receives everything as an emotional experience, a man must be sensitive about her feelings, considering his words rather than saying whatever comes to his mind.

On the other hand, a woman needs to realize that when she talks to a man, he hears it only as information. He runs on information because he's a logical thinker. When she wants to talk to a man, she has to learn to tell him what she thinks, not what she feels. Sometimes a woman will become upset at something that a man has done and will start crying. A woman needs to release her emotions, and she often expresses them through tears. However, the man says, "I'm going to leave. I'll come back when you've settled down and we can talk." To the woman, he's being cold. What he's really saying is, "I'm looking for information, and I'm not receiving any." The man doesn't want her tears because he doesn't know how to respond to them. He feels sorry that she is crying, but he wants to know what he can do to fix things. He wants information. The woman can recognize this and respond in a way that he will receive.

⌒

*Thought*: What a woman hears, she receives as an emotional experience; what a man hears, he generally receives as information.

*Readings*: Psalm 44:1–3; Mark 4:1–20

# HIDDEN THOUGHTS AND FEELINGS

*"Clothe yourselves with compassion, kindness, humility, gentleness and patience. Bear with each other...."*
—Colossians 3:12–13

A woman is likely to express what she feels rather than what she thinks, especially at first. For example, when a woman is under stress and wants someone to empathize with her so that she doesn't feel so alone in her difficulty, she may say something like this to her husband: "Your parents are coming for dinner tomorrow, the house is a mess, we don't have any groceries, the kids have been underfoot all day, and I just can't do it all!" Her husband, who is a thinker, will immediately try to come up with a solution for his distraught wife. "Well, what if I go buy some groceries?" "No, I have to do that tomorrow when I know what I want to cook." "Then why don't I take you and the kids out to dinner so you won't have to worry about that tonight?" "No, we can't be out late. The kids need baths, and, besides, I have to use up the leftovers." "Well, then, let me straighten things up a little." "No, I need to do that. I know where everything belongs."

By now, the man is totally exasperated because he is trying to help his wife, but she is rejecting all his suggestions. He doesn't realize that what the woman really wants is for him to take her in his arms and tell her how much she is appreciated. While she would also probably appreciate his help, she first needs emotional contact with him. Then, the other problems won't seem as insurmountable. What she was *thinking* was that she could handle things if she received some love and affection from her husband. What she *expressed* were her overwhelming feelings of overload, which her husband interpreted as a need for him to solve her problems by taking action.

In contrast, most of the time, when a man speaks to a woman, he doesn't communicate what he's *feeling*. The misunderstanding this causes contributes to problems in relationships. It can be difficult for women to understand how very hard it is for men to express their feelings. Yet it is very important for a woman not to jump to any conclusions about a man's motivations until she discovers what he is feeling.

There are many men who are feeling emotions they find difficult to verbalize. They are hurting; they feel sad and weak inside. They feel like losers. They are depressed that they haven't been promoted for ten years and that nothing is working out with their jobs. They feel as if they have failed their wives. They feel bad, but it is hard for them to come up with the words to express these feelings.

To help a man overcome any embarrassment he has about his feelings and learn to communicate those feelings, a woman needs to create an environment that will enable him to tell her what he is feeling.

*Thought*: It is very important for a woman not to jump to any conclusions about a man's motivations until she discovers what he is feeling.

*Readings*: Psalm 38:9; 1 Peter 5:7

# DIFFERENCES IN PROBLEM SOLVING

*"Speaking the truth in love, we will grow to become in every respect the mature body of him who is the head, that is, Christ."*                                    —Ephesians 4:15

Women and men's distinct approaches to problem solving often cause them to react differently to life's difficulties or to conflicts in interpersonal relationships.

Men generally are like filing cabinets: they make decisions quickly and "file" them away in their minds. Or, they put a problem in a mental "to do" folder and go on to other things. They reopen the folder only when they feel ready to deal with it. In contrast, women generally are like computers. Their minds keep working things through until a problem is solved.

Men tend to be resentful about problems, and it's harder for them to see past their anger. They might just "file away" their problems and ignore them for a while. On the other hand, women are guilt-prone; therefore, they often feel responsible for these situations, whether they have caused them or not. Even if they are angry, they will look within to see what they could have done differently or how they can resolve the situation.

Men and women can eliminate much frustration in their relationships by understanding each other's problem-solving strengths and using them to benefit one another. For instance, a woman can assist a man in resolving a problem with a coworker by talking through the difficulty with him and helping him to recognize the motivations and feelings involved. A man can help a woman reach a decision more quickly by acknowledging her feelings about a situation but also clearly outlining for her the facts and options involved. Taking into consideration both intuitive and factual information will help women and men to make better decisions.

⌒

*Thought*: Different approaches to problem solving often are the reason women and men will react differently to life's difficulties or conflicts in interpersonal relationships.

*Readings*: Proverbs 2:6; James 1:5–6

# DIFFERENCES IN REALIZING GOALS

*"From* [Christ] *the whole body, joined and held together by every supporting ligament, grows and builds itself up in love, as each part does its work."* —Ephesians 4:16

When it comes to material things, such as a job task, a building project, or financial planning, men want to know the details of how to get there. They like to know what steps they must take to achieve a task. In contrast, women tend to look at overall goals. They think about what they want to accomplish rather than focusing on a step-by-step outline of what needs to be done. While a man will sit down and write out a list of points, a woman might just start doing something to make sure it gets done.

However, when it comes to spiritual or intangible things, the opposite is generally true: males look at overall goals, while females want to know how to get there. These tendencies are why men usually remember the gist of a matter, while women often remember the details and overlook the gist. Men are interested in the principle, the abstract, the philosophy. They see the general direction they need to go in spiritually, and they head toward it. As long as they know what they believe, they don't always see the need for activities designed to help them arrive at their goal. However, women like to be involved in the process. They will attend prayer meetings and Bible studies, read Christian books, and participate more in the life of the church because it will help them grow spiritually.

Men and women can bring balance to one another in both material and spiritual things by helping each other to keep visions and goals clearly in mind while identifying the steps that are necessary to accomplish them effectively.

<hr>

*Thought*: When it comes to spiritual things, males look at overall goals, while females want to know how to get there. Men see the general direction they need to go in, while women like to be involved in the process.

*Readings*: Proverbs 3:5–6; Philippians 3:12–14

# DIFFERENCES IN PERSONALITY AND SELF-PERCEPTION

*"Love is patient, love is kind. It does not envy, it does not boast, it is not proud. It does not dishonor others, it is not self-seeking, it is not easily angered, it keeps no record of wrongs. Love does not delight in evil but rejoices with the truth. It always protects, always trusts, always hopes, always perseveres."*
—1 Corinthians 13:4–7

A man's job is an extension of his personality, whereas a woman's home is an extension of hers. This difference can cause much conflict in relationships. A woman may want her husband to spend time with her at home, but he can enjoy working twelve hours a day away from the home because he's cultivating something that is a reflection of who he is. When a man loses his job, it can be devastating to his self-esteem because he considers his job to be almost synonymous with himself.

A woman places high value on her physical surroundings and on creating a home. Men don't understand why women become upset when they track sawdust in the living room after it has just been vacuumed. Men are not trying to be inconsiderate; they just don't think in the same terms that women do. When the beauty and order of the home are disturbed, it can be unsettling for a woman.

Another aspect of the differences in male and female personality is that men's personalities are fairly consistent, while women are continually changing. Women seek personal growth and development more than men do. They like to redecorate the home, discover new skills, or gain a new outlook. Men are often satisfied to follow the same routines, think in the same patterns, and wear the same suits—for twenty years!

Understanding these differences in personality traits is essential because they involve sensitive areas of our lives, such as what we value and how we perceive ourselves. Women and men can use their knowledge of these distinctions to build up each another's self-esteem and to give each other latitude when they view life differently.

*Thought*: Women often seek personal growth and development while men are often satisfied to follow the same routines.

*Readings*: Genesis 2:8–15; 2 Peter 3:18

# DIFFERENCES IN IDEAS OF SECURITY AND COMFORT

*"God is our refuge and strength, an ever-present help in trouble. Therefore we will not fear, though the earth give way and the mountains fall into the heart of the sea, though its waters roar and foam and the mountains quake with their surging."*
—Psalm 46:1–3

Because men put a strong emphasis on their jobs and are not as emotionally connected to their physical surroundings, they have a tendency to be nomadic as they look for new career opportunities. Conversely, many women have a great need for security and roots. While a move due to a new job seems like an adventure for a man and signals progress in his career, it can be stressful and difficult for his wife, who may have to leave family and friends behind for an uncertain future. Women will also change geographic locations for jobs; however, married women are less willing to make a move to advance their own jobs than they are for their husbands' jobs. They are less inclined to want to disrupt the lives of their families, especially when they have children.

On the other hand, when it comes to encountering something new, men tend to stand back and evaluate at first. Women are more ready to accept new experiences, and they participate in them more easily.

Matters involving security and comfort can require great understanding on the part of a spouse. They reflect issues such as fulfillment, trustworthiness, fear, and feelings of instability. When men or women want to make job changes or embark on something new, they should be aware of the possible reactions of their spouses and show kindness and patience as they work through these potential changes to their lives.

⌒

*Thought*: Matters involving security and comfort can require great understanding on the part of a spouse because they reflect issues such as fulfillment, trustworthiness, fear, and feelings of instability.

*Readings*: Psalm 46; Romans 15:13

— *Day 73* —

# SEE THE VISION

*"Where there is no vision, the people perish."*
—Proverbs 29:18 (KJV)

While purpose is why you were born, vision is when you start seeing it yourself. Vision is necessary for life. The word *"vision"* in the Hebrew means a "dream, revelation, or oracle." Obviously, a vision that is connected to God's purposes is something that needs to be revealed by God Himself. You need His revelation of your life's vision. The only way you can discover this vision is to listen to what God is saying to you.

To have vision is to be able to conceive of and move toward your purpose in life. While God does want us to wait for His guidance and direction, He doesn't want us to abuse this principle by not earnestly seeking His particular vision and plan for us.

The greatest example of someone who had a vision for His life is Jesus. He constantly repeated and affirmed who He was. Jesus knew His identity as the Son of God and as God the Son. He knew His reason for being and His purpose in life. (See, for example, John 8:58; Luke 19:10.)

The example Jesus set for us shows us our need for these important elements related to purpose: (1) a clear self-image and (2) a life consistent with one's purpose and calling. Jesus lived a life that was totally consistent with who He said He was. He had complete integrity; He always kept and fulfilled His own words.

Vision is the capacity to see beyond your physical eyes into a preferred future. Vision is purpose in pictures. Have you been seeing pictures of your dream? Perhaps your dreams are being drowned out by your music, your phone, and other people talking. When you turn off the TV and computer and everything is quiet, do you start thinking of your future? In the Bible, whenever God wanted to speak to someone about their work, He always took them away from other people. God took Abraham to a mountain all by himself. He took Moses to the desert. David heard from God when he was out tending sheep in the hills. You need to disengage from the noise of life so you can see pictures of your future.

Purpose produces a vision, and a vision produces a plan. Once there's a plan, it produces discipline in you. Write down your purpose and vision, and then get some pictures symbolizing that vision and what you need to fulfill it. I cut out pictures of my dream and put them where I could see them every day. I would say, "That's what I'm going to do."

*"Many are the plans in a person's heart, but it is the Lord's purpose that prevails"* (Proverbs 19:21). I want this Scripture to be emblazoned on your heart. God's purpose for your life is already established; He's not worried about your future. Whatever you were born to do is already finished in Him. Cease worrying about it, capture His vision for your life, and start making plans to go there.

⌣‿⌐

*Thought*: Capture God's vision for your life and start making plans to go there.

*Readings*: Habakkuk 2:2–3; 2 Timothy 2:20–21

# WHAT IS YOUR DREAM?

*"I know the plans I have for you,"* declares the LORD, *"plans to prosper you and not to harm you, plans to give you hope and a future."* —Jeremiah 29:11

Having a vision is inherent in being human. Maybe you once had ideas of what you wanted to be and do, and you still have those ideas. Do you see yourself becoming a lawyer and starting your own firm? Do you think about owning a day-care center that has a first-class curriculum and services two hundred children? Do you want to write a novel? Do you dream about going back to school and doing something with your education and academic abilities?

I have come to the conclusion that the poorest person in the world is the person without a dream. A dream, or vision, provides us with direction. It has been said that if you don't know where you're going, any road will take you there. We don't want to end up on just any road in life.

While the poorest person in the world is the one without a dream, the most frustrated person in the world is someone who has a dream but doesn't know how to bring it to pass. Yet if you can have hope for the future, you have true riches, no matter how much money you have in your bank account. It doesn't matter what you currently have or don't have, as long as you can see what you could have. This vision is the key to life because where there's a dream, there's hope, and where there's hope, there's faith—and faith is the substance, or fulfillment, of what you are hoping for. (See Hebrews 11:1.)

I encourage you to believe in your daydreams and to reconnect with your passion; your vision awaits your action. Your future is not ahead of you—it lies within you. See beyond your eyes and live for the unseen. Your vision determines your destiny. God truly has plans for you.

*Thought:* Vision generates hope and provides endurance in difficult times.

*Readings:* Psalm 37:3–4; 1 Thessalonians 1:3

# THE WORLD CAN'T FORGET

*"Whatever you do, work at it with all your heart, as working for the Lord."* —Colossians 3:23

Every human being was created to accomplish something specific that no one else can accomplish. You were designed to be known for something special. You are meant to do something that will make you unforgettable. You were born to do something that the world will not be able to ignore. It may be in your church, your community, your state, or beyond.

The Bible is a great book for recording the stories of people who did little things that the world can't forget. In the New Testament, there is the story of the woman who took an alabaster jar of perfume and anointed Jesus's head with it. This woman was taking a chance by violating the accepted social code of the day and interrupting a group of men who had gathered for a meal. She decided to pour out her life in gratitude to Jesus, no matter what the consequences. Some of those present severely criticized her because she had "wasted" costly perfume on Jesus when it could have been sold for charitable purposes. Yet Jesus said to them, *"Leave her alone.... Truly I tell you, wherever the gospel is preached throughout the world, what she has done will also be told, in memory of her"* (Mark 14:6, 9). No matter how small the act may be, if you put your whole life into it, it won't be forgotten.

Agnes Gonxha Bojaxhiu, whom the world came to know as Mother Teresa, felt her life's purpose was to serve God full-time. When she was eighteen, she became a nun and went to India with the Sisters of Loreto and taught in a Catholic high school for many years. Her life's purpose and passion crystallized as she felt called by God to help "the poorest of the poor" and devoted herself to bring hope, dignity, healing, and education to the needy in Calcutta—those whom other people dismissed as being either beyond help or not worthy of it.

Mother Teresa started her own order called "The Missionaries of Charity" and became internationally recognized for her selfless humanitarian work. Her passion to help others led her to identify totally with them: she became a citizen of India and always kept her vow of poverty, even when she became famous. Her work expanded beyond India to other nations of the world, influencing hundreds of thousands of people to join in her vision. She believed in the difference that one person could make in the world, saying, "If you can't feed a hundred people, then just feed one." Mother Teresa was awarded the Nobel Peace Prize in 1979 and continued her work until her death in 1997.

Mother Teresa encouraged others not to wait for well-known leaders to do a job but to follow their visions. By acting when there was a real need and doing what she personally could do to help, Mother Teresa became a leader herself. She influenced numerous others to awaken their own visionary gifts and, in so doing, multiplied her effectiveness thousands of times over.

~

*Thought*: Every human being was created to accomplish something specific that no one else can accomplish.

*Readings*: Jeremiah 1:4–5; Romans 11:29

# KNOWN FOR YOUR VISION

*"For it is God who works in you to will and to act in order to fulfill his good purpose."*　　　　　—Philippians 2:13

The very substance of life is for you to find God's purpose and fulfill it. Until you do that, you are not really living. You need to make sure you can say at the end of your life, as Jesus did, *"It is finished"* (John 19:30) and not just, "I am retired," for your dream is much bigger than mere retirement.

Are you in your twenties? What have you done so far with your life? Have you spent so much time trying to please your friends that you don't know who you are or what your life is about? If so, you aren't doing yourself any favors. You aren't fulfilling your purpose. You may say you are just reacting to "peer pressure." In reality, you are allowing others to rule your life.

Maybe you are forty years old. What have you done so far that the world can't forget? How long will you drift along without working toward your dream? Be careful—procrastination can become a full-time occupation! Many people spend a lifetime wandering away from who God made them to be because they have never recognized who they are in the first place. For example, perhaps you have been a secretary for twenty years. You are at the same level as when you started, even though you dream of being an administrator. People don't fulfill their visions because they have no sense of destiny.

We need to be like the apostles, who were known for their acts, not their talk. The biblical book about them is called The Acts of the Apostles because they were doers. They were affecting government. They were transforming the world. Nations were afraid of them, and towns became nervous when they showed up because they were said to have *"turned the world upside down"* (Acts 17:6 NKJV). It's exciting to be around people who know that they are doing what they were born to do. You should be known for your God-given vision, too.

⌒

*Thought:* The very substance of life is for you to find God's purpose and fulfill it.

*Readings:* 1 Peter 4:10–11; Acts 9:36–41

# VISION IS UNSELFISH

*"Do nothing out of selfish ambition or vain conceit. Rather, in humility value others above yourselves, not looking to your own interests but each of you to the interests of the others."*
—Philippians 2:3–4

True vision is unselfish. Its purpose is to bring God's kingdom on earth and turn people to Him. A vision should always focus on helping humanity or building up others in some way.

First, this means that God will never have you pursue your vision at the expense of your family. A beloved friend of mine went to a conference where a supposed prophet spoke to him about what God wanted for his life. He came to me and asked, "Did you hear what the prophet said? What do you think?" I replied, "Well, let's pray over that prophecy. Let's take our time, get counsel, and find God's will on it." However, the next time I heard from him, he had already set up a plan to fulfill this prophecy. He went to another country, leaving behind a confused and angry family. Was this really God's purpose?

There are instances when family members will agree to be apart for a time to serve a certain purpose. Moreover, your family will not always understand or support your dream. Yet pursuing it shouldn't destroy their lives. Vision should always be accompanied by compassion.

Second, a true vision will not take the form of building a big business just so you can have millions of dollars for expensive homes and cars. These things may be goals, but they are not vision—in fact, they are probably selfish ambition because they build your kingdom rather than God's kingdom. Your vision might well involve making a large amount of money. The difference, however, is in your motivation and attitude. You need to treat your finances as a resource God has provided to fulfill your vision, not as a tool to fill your life with luxuries.

I invite you to pray the following prayer:

Father, I know that You want me to pursue my life's dreams with compassion for others. Please keep me from selfish motives. In Jesus's name, amen.

*Thought*: Vision's purpose is to bring about God's kingdom on earth.

*Readings*: Proverbs 11:25; James 3:13–18

# GOD SENT A WOMAN

*"I brought you up from the land of Egypt, I redeemed you from the house of bondage; and I sent before you Moses, Aaron, and Miriam."* —Micah 6:4 (NKJV)

Women should take the above verse to heart and remember it for the rest of their lives. God was saying, "I sent you three leaders." We always talk about Moses, the representative and administrative leader. We also talk about Aaron, the high priest and spiritual leader. But God mentioned another leader that many people are uncomfortable reading about. He said, "I also sent Miriam to lead you."

God *sent* a woman to lead. This fact contradicts many of the attitudes that men have had for years about women in leadership. When God purposefully appointed Miriam to be a leader to His people, He endorsed the idea that it is valid for a woman to be in leadership. It is noteworthy that God did not send Miriam to lead because no men were available at the time. Rather, He sent her to lead *alongside* the men. He put her in a team of leaders. Since God acknowledged Miriam in the same list or category with Moses, we don't have to question whether God intended women to be leaders. *"I sent before you Moses, Aaron, and Miriam."*

The Sinai leadership team included a director, a priest, and a woman. The director was Moses, the executive leader; the priest was Aaron, the spiritual leader. Yet right in the middle of the executive leader and the spiritual leader, a woman was needed in order to bring balance to both of them.

Miriam's influential role as a leader over Israel looks *back* to God's purposes for the woman that He established when He created humanity and *ahead* to Christ's redemptive purposes for the woman in salvation. God intended women to be leaders from the creation of the world, and He confirmed His continued commitment to this intention through the ministry of His Son Jesus Christ.

Throughout our exploration of God's purposes for men and women and male-female relationships, we have seen the following:

+ Women and men (as man) are spiritually equal before God and equally as important to Him.
+ Women and men (as man) were given the dominion mandate.
+ Males and females (man's "houses") have distinct purposes and designs.
+ The complementary roles and abilities of males and females bring balance, strength, and help to one another as they fulfill God's purposes.

In light of these principles, the question many people have been asking, "Should women be in leadership?" becomes an entirely different question. Instead of asking *if* women should be in leadership, we should be asking *how* they are to exercise their leadership, given their purpose and design. In our next devotionals, we will explore how the woman's purpose and design shape her leadership role.

*Thought*: God intended women to be leaders from the creation of the world.

*Readings*: Genesis 1:26–27; Ephesians 4:11–13

# DESIGNED TO LEAD

*"God created man in his own image, in the image of God he created them; male and female he created them. God blessed them and said to them, "Be fruitful and increase in number; fill the earth and subdue it. Rule ["have dominion" NKJV, KJV] over the fish in the sea and the birds in the sky and over every living creature that moves on the ground."*
—Genesis 1:27–28 (NIV84)

Consider once more that the creation account reveals that the dominion mandate was given to "man," both male and female. It is God's purpose that the woman, as well as the man, be fruitful and multiply, replenish, subdue, and have dominion over the earth. To have dominion means to govern, rule, control, manage, lead, or administrate. *Dominion* is a powerful word. God loves leadership and had it in mind when He created the earth. When God told man to have dominion, He was telling man who he is. Man (male and female) is a leader who is to cultivate the earth.

There is no incidence of subjection or oppression of women in the first and second chapters of Genesis. In God's perfect will, there is no such arrangement. The woman and the man were both equal, blessed, subduing, ruling, and having dominion, and God said, "This is very good." Any other arrangement than this was the result of the fall. This means that anything that God said about the male-female relationship after Genesis 2 is a repair program.

Since God's purpose for mankind was leadership, He designed male and female with the built-in potential and ability to be leaders. The leadership spirit is in every person. However, the ways in which males and females *execute* dominion are different based on their distinct designs.

⌒

*Thought*: God designed both male and female with the built-in potential and ability to be leaders; the leadership spirit is in every person.

*Readings*: Psalm 8; Revelation 1:4–6

# THE INFLUENCE-POWER OF WOMEN

*"She speaks with wisdom, and faithful instruction is on her tongue."*                    —Proverbs 31:26

Both the man and the woman were created to lead, but their leadership functions are determined by their specific dominion assignments. God designed the woman not only for relationship with Himself, but also to help fulfill His purposes in His great plan for humanity. Therefore, women are designed by God to execute an assignment that can be fulfilled only by them.

God designed the male to be a leader by position and the female to be a leader by influence. Thus, the man has *position-power* and the woman has *influence-power*. There is a difference between these two forms of leadership. A perfect example of this distinction was Queen Esther's position in relation to King Xerxes. The king had position-power. Yet because of Esther's godly heart and her great beauty, she had influence-power with the king and was able to convince him of Haman's evil plans against the Jewish people.

When God designed the female, He obviously had influence in mind. A woman is a receiver. God designed her to receive from the male and to incubate what she receives so that it can grow and develop. A woman is built to influence. Her wombs—whether physical, emotional, mental, or spiritual—have a tremendous influence on what they receive by providing a nurturing and transforming environment. There is much truth in William Ross Wallace's famous quote: "The hand that rocks the cradle is the hand that rules the world."

Position-power and influence-power are not mutually exclusive; they are meant to be exercised together in dominion. For example, God gave the woman a way of thinking that is amazing. If you take a little thought, a little idea, and drop it into a woman's mind, you'll never get that simple idea back—you'll get a fully developed plan.

Do you know why many men turn the running of the home over to their wives? A woman can take a mortgage that's overdue or a business that's falling apart and say, "You sit down; let me handle this." She knows how to get a man through these things. She can dig him out of a hole. The sad thing is that when some men get out of the hole, they proceed to walk over their wives. The unique qualities and contributions of women must be valued by men.

⌣‿⌐

*Thought*: The man has *position-power*, and the woman has *influence-power*.

*Readings*: Book of Esther; Luke 8:1–3

# DISTINCT LEADERSHIP FUNCTIONS

*"She sees that her trading is profitable, and her lamp does not
go out at night…. She opens her arms to the poor and extends
her hands to the needy."* —Proverbs 31:18, 20

Power and influence are equal but different. A woman and a
man are equal in leadership. The difference is in their leadership
functions.

There are two important aspects of position-power. First,
position-power generally comes with a title, such as king, gover-
nor, or pastor. Second, position-power is usually executed through
commands, whether verbal or written. It is the authority that goes
with the position—and underlies the commands—that is the
nature of the man's power.

Influence-power manifests itself in a very different way. First,
a woman may have a title, but she doesn't need a title in order to
lead. She leads by influence. Men call themselves "the head of the
house," but the women run the homes. Second, a woman doesn't
need to talk in order to run things. She leads just by her influence.
My father used to run our household with his mouth. He would
say, "Take your feet off that chair." However, my mother would just
*look* at me, and my feet would be down off that chair. The woman
doesn't need to say a word; she just looks, and people respond. This
is a powerful influence. Some men assume that because certain
women are quiet or don't bark out orders, they are weak. They do
not understand influence-power.

Influence-power may be more subtle and quiet than position-power, but it has a potent effect. Satan understood this

influence. The fall of man resulted from the serpent's interference with influence leadership.

Influence-power is a tremendous gift from God that was intended to be used by women for the good of themselves, their families, their communities, their nations, the world, and the kingdom of God. Yet women have to realize its potential for evil as well as for good. Even redeemed women have to be careful to discipline their influence-power.

Even though the woman's influence-power has the potential to harm, it was God who originally gave her this leadership gift when He created her. The *influence* is not the result of the fall; the *corruption* of the influence is. God desires that the woman be restored to her full leadership role and use this influence for His good purposes. God indicated that this was His plan even at the time of the fall. He said that in the end, He was going to restore what He had established in the beginning. How? Through the redemption of Jesus Christ and the coming of the Holy Spirit.

When the Holy Spirit comes back into a woman's life, God's plan for her reverts to what it was originally. Women are joint and equal heirs of salvation with men. This means that when a woman receives salvation in Jesus Christ, she becomes equal in rulership again.

⌒

*Thought*: God desires that the woman be restored to her full leadership role and use her influence-power for His good purposes.

*Readings*: 1 Samuel 25:2–35; Mark 6:17–29

# A TRUSTED LEADER

*"All authority in heaven and on earth has been given to me.
Therefore go and make disciples of all nations."*
—Matthew 28:18–19

When Jesus was about to ascend to heaven, He told His followers, in effect, "I have to return to My Father, but I want to influence the world for My kingdom. I am the King and I am the Word; therefore, I exercise position-power. To influence the world, I need a wife, a partner, who has influence-power."

Christ left the earth in the hands of a "woman," the church. Being a member of the body of Christ means not only receiving salvation, but also helping the Lord in His purpose of winning the world to Himself. This is why He gave the church the responsibility of going into the world as a witness for Him. Christ sees her as a perfect leader, and He shows this by the fact that He has entrusted the Word of God to her.

Now, the implication is that the female is a trusted leader, just as the male is. The church is not the servant of Jesus, just as the female is not the servant of the male; she is his partner. Jesus said to His disciples, *"I no longer call you servants.... Instead, I have called you friends, for everything that I learned from my Father I have made known to you"* (John 15:15).

Jesus also told the church, in effect, "You will be seated *with* Me in heavenly places." (See Ephesians 2:6.) He did not say, "You will be seated *below* Me." Since Christ is the King, the church is His queen. We need to see God's intent for the female in this portrayal of Christ and the church. She is not meant to sit below the male but to be his partner in leadership, in dominion.

⁓

*Thought*: We need to see God's leadership intent for the female in the Scriptures' portrayal of Christ and the church.

*Readings*: Isaiah 9:6–7; Ephesians 2:4–10

*— Day 83 —*

# WHAT ABOUT PAUL?

*"There is neither Jew nor Gentile, neither slave nor free, nor is there male and female, for you are all one in Christ Jesus."*
                                                              —Galatians 3:28

When Paul wrote the above statement to the Galatians, he was talking about the spirit-man that resides in both males and females whom Christ has redeemed. In other letters, such as those to Corinth and Ephesus, Paul addressed problems in which people's cultural heritages were making it difficult for them to adjust to their new Christian faith. For example, he told the Corinthians, *"Women should remain silent in the churches. They are not allowed to speak, but must be in submission, as the law says"* (1 Corinthians 14:34).

This passage has been terribly misunderstood and has been used as a general rule in order to keep women down, to subjugate and oppress them. Many people don't realize that, in the same letter, Paul gave instructions to women who pray or prophesy in the church. (See 1 Corinthians 11:5.) Obviously, they needed to speak in order to do that. Therefore, I believe that Paul's instructions to the Corinthians had to do with keeping order in the churches when the people's carnality or cultural backgrounds were creating confusion and discord. God is a God of order. Based on Paul's other writings, as well as additional passages and biblical principles from both the Old and New Testaments, these few instructions of Paul's should not be considered the sole or final word on the matter.

Which is more important, culture or Christ? Did Jesus ever command a woman to be silent? Did Jesus ever stop a woman from preaching? Remember that the woman at the well began preaching after Jesus set her free, and then she became an evangelist. (See John 4:4–30.)

Sometimes we make Paul's statement in 1 Corinthians 14:34, *"Women should remain silent in the churches,"* more important than Jesus's own revelation of God's purposes. *Please do not misunderstand what I am saying. It is all God's Word.* Yet I truly believe that Paul was dealing with specific cultural issues; Christ was dealing with principles. Culture should not be confused with principles. Jesus elevated, promoted, and restored women to their original dignity. Moreover, Paul himself affirmed the female's equality with the male in Christ.

Even before Jesus died on the cross, He affirmed women in His earthly ministry in a way that was revolutionary to fallen man but was right in line with God's purposes for man in creation. This was a striking illustration of His respect for women and their value to Him, their Creator and Redeemer.

Therefore, it is not only the male, but also the female, who can be a leader. Their leadership styles do not cancel each other out; it is the *combination* of position-power and influence-power that enables man to exercise dominion over the world, and which will bring the kingdom of God on earth. The devil is in trouble when the two types of power come together in unity of purpose.

⌒

*Thought*: Jesus elevated, promoted, and restored women to their original dignity.

*Readings*: 2 Chronicles 34:14–33; Galatians 3:26–29

# WOULD YOU LIKE UNFADING BEAUTY?

*"Your beauty…should be that of your inner self, the unfading beauty of a gentle and quiet spirit, which is of great worth in God's sight."* —1 Peter 3:3–4

First Peter 3:4 says that a woman's beauty *"should be that of [her] inner self."* It is this *"inner self"* that is a woman's spirit. What the woman is physically is different from what she is in her inner self. We have seen that, spiritually, both men and women have the same spirit-man within. The spirit-man inside every woman is the being that relates to God. Jesus said, *"God is spirit, and his worshipers must worship in the Spirit and in truth"* (John 4:24). A woman has her own spirit-being with which to worship God. She can bless the Lord and love the Lord and receive from the Lord herself. A woman who loves and worships the Lord and reflects His nature has unfading beauty in God's sight.

In order for a woman to become what God intends, she needs to be filled with the Holy Spirit, submitted to the Word, and learning to follow the leading of the Spirit. You must develop an ongoing, intimate relationship with God. For instance, you can't just read popular women's magazines or watch talk shows and expect to get revelation from God. These sources are usually headed deeper and deeper into the wilderness. They're leading you into perversion and depravity. The wilderness mentality of women is, "I don't need anybody else. I'm going to make it on my own. I don't care what anyone says; I don't need any man." I believe you know that's wilderness talk because, deep inside, you have a garden desire. You need to be in relationship with God, and you need to be in relationship with men—with a husband or with your brothers in the Lord—in order to be who you were created to be.

This is the ideal, and God wants you to work back to it. He wants you to have the spirit of the garden so that you will be in continual fellowship with Him. Then you will be able to experience fulfillment both as a spiritual being created in God's image, and as a female, created for God's good purposes.

⌒

*Thought*: In order for a woman to become what God intends, she needs to be filled with the Holy Spirit, submitted to the Word, and learning to follow the leading of the Spirit.

*Readings*: Proverbs 11:16; Galatians 5:24–25

# PRAYER IS ESSENTIAL FOR GOD'S WILL

*"For Yours is the kingdom and the power and the glory forever."* —Matthew 6:13 (NKJV)

As human beings, our need to pray results from the way God arranged dominion on the earth. God made the world. Then He made men and women, giving them dominion over the works of His hands. When God said, *"Let them rule…over all the earth"* (Genesis 1:26 NIV84), He ordered the dominion of the world in a way that made rule by humans essential to accomplishing His purposes. He causes things to happen on earth when men and women are in agreement with His will. Prayer, therefore, is essential for God's will to be done in the earth. Since God never breaks His Word concerning how things are to work, prayer is mandatory, not optional, for spiritual progress.

God's plan is for mankind to desire what He desires, to will what He wills, and to ask Him to accomplish His purposes in the world so that goodness and truth, rather than evil and darkness, may reign on the earth. In this sense, by praying, we give God the freedom to intervene in earth's affairs.

Even before God's plan of redemption was fully accomplished in Christ, God used humans to fulfill His will. We see this truth in the lives of Abraham, Moses, Gideon, David, Daniel, and many others. God continued to work with mankind to fulfill His purposes on earth even though man's part was limited by his sin and lack of understanding of God's ways.

As a man or woman created in the image of God, dominion authority is your heritage. God desires that you will His will. His will should be the foundation of your prayers, the heart of your intercession, and the source of your confidence in supplication.

When we know and obey God's will, and ask Him to fulfill it, He will grant our request. Whether we are praying for individual, family, community, national, or world needs, we must seek to be in agreement with God's will so His purposes can reign on the earth. This is the essence of exercising dominion.

*Thought:* God causes things to happen on earth when men and women are in agreement with His will.

*Readings:* Isaiah 55:10–11; Matthew 6:5–14

# THE IMPORTANCE OF FORGIVENESS

*"Therefore, if you are offering your gift at the altar and there remember that your brother or sister has something against you, leave your gift there in front of the altar. First go and be reconciled to them; then come and offer your gift."*

—Matthew 5:23–24

Jesus talked a great deal about the importance of forgiveness in our relationships. He said that if you do not forgive someone who has something against you, or whom you have something against, then the Father will not forgive you and will not hear you. Jesus was saying that relationships with other people are even more important than worship, because you cannot worship except in the context of your relationships.

It doesn't matter how serious and sincere you are about God. It doesn't matter how filled you are with the Holy Spirit or how much Scripture you've learned. God is not overly impressed by your ability to communicate with Him, by your ability to articulate your worship, prayer, or praise. His reception of your worship—whether it is through your giving, your praise, your administration of the kingdom of God, or your ministry of the gifts of the Spirit—is contingent upon your relationships with others, especially your spouse. So, if you give God a thousand dollars, whether or not God receives it depends on whether or not you are in right relationship with others. God's acceptance of even your tithes is contingent upon your relationships with other people, not on how much you give Him.

Thus, a right relationship with God is dependent on right relationships with other people. This truth brings the matter of reconciled relationships between women and men down to where it hurts, doesn't it? We must understand clearly what God's Word says so that we have no excuse for failing to mend our broken relationships.

Can you imagine husbands and wives stopping in the middle of Sunday morning worship and stepping outside to make things right with each other? If that were to happen, we'd have a brand new church and society. Yet I find that people often try the easy route when they have been in conflict with others. They go to God and say, "God, please forgive Mary," "God, tell Mary that I forgive her," or "God, I ask You to change Mary." They don't want to go to the person directly. We love to hide behind God so we don't have to accept the responsibility of face-to-face relationships. Our reluctance to deal honestly and directly with others is the reason why there are so many problems in relationships, even in the body of Christ.

I honor my wife and do right by her, not only because I love her, but also for the sake of my relationship with God. "*Husbands,… be considerate as you live with your wives…so that nothing will hinder your prayers*" (1 Peter 3:7). Jesus said that my relationship with God is even more important than my relationship with my wife— and yet God made my relationship with Him contingent on my relationship with her.

⌒

*Thought*: You cannot worship God except in the context of your relationships.

*Readings*: Genesis 50:15–21; Mark 11:24–25

# PREPARED FOR THE STORM

*"The eternal God is your refuge, and underneath are the everlasting arms."*　　　　　—Deuteronomy 33:27

To everything there is a season, a time for every purpose under heaven" (Ecclesiastes 3:1 NKJV). Everything in life has a season. This means that whatever difficulties we're experiencing are not going to last. However, it also means that whatever we are enjoying now may not last, either. Many of us do not want to hear this; we think that everything is forever.

You are not to trust in the permanence of anything on earth except for your relationship with God. Parents, friends, coworkers, pastors, church members—they're all for a season. Be prepared for the season of living without them. We must have our anchor on the Rock because the Rock has no season—He is eternal.

Let me remind you that even if you are in Christ Jesus, you are not immune to storms. When we look at people who are men and women of God, who are faithful in service to Him, who are praying people, or who have served others greatly, but who still find themselves in crises, we say, "This isn't supposed to happen to people like them." As Jesus indicated in one of His parables, it doesn't matter what kind of "house" you have—whether built on sand or rock—the storm is coming. The issue is not really the storm. The issue is the foundation. Remember that as you hold on to the Rock, your foundation will remain sure. (See Matthew 7:24–27.)

I've lived in the Bahamas all my life, and God has used the ocean to teach me essential lessons on Christian living. Often, my friends and I have gone out on our boats early in the morning to fish, and the water is like glass as we speed over the ocean. By one o'clock in the afternoon, however, a storm may be coming, and, since we're ten miles from shore, we have to start tying everything down. The season has changed, and the boat will rock during the storm, but everyone knows what to do. We've already been trained; we've prepared for the storm.

We know to put the anchor down. We actually dive down and put that anchor under the rock. Then, we brace everything. When the storm is upon us, it's too late to do anything else; the season has come. We're beaten about by the wind and waves, but after about fifteen or twenty minutes, it passes us by. Then, it's peaceful again, and we can go back to fishing.

It will be the same with you. Once you have committed to the Rock and have prepared for the changing seasons of life, you will be able to ride out the storm and then go back to fishing. It's going to be all right, and it's going to be even better fishing because the storm will have stirred up more fish. Behind every broken experience is a wealthy experience from the Lord. There is peace in the promise that nothing earthly lasts, but the Rock is eternal.

⌒

*Thought*: You are not immune to storms. Are you holding on to the Rock?

*Readings*: Psalm 62:5–8; Matthew 7:24–27

# REFLECTING GOD'S NATURE
# TO THE WORLD

*"There are also celestial bodies and terrestrial bodies; but the glory of the celestial is one, and the glory of the terrestrial is another. There is one glory of the sun, another glory of the moon, and another glory of the stars; for one star differs from another star in glory."* —1 Corinthians 15:40–41 (NKJV)

When we think of *"glory,"* we often think of a cloud filled with light. Yet glory in the sense of the above passage has to do with the nature of something. In its larger meaning, the word *glory* can be ascribed to every single thing. *The glory of something is its best expression of itself.*

One of the definitions of *glory* is "a distinguished quality or asset." You can see a flower in its true glory when it is in full bloom. You can see a leopard or a lion in its true glory when it is at its prime strength. You can see the sun in its true glory at twelve noon; after that, its light begins to fade. The glory of a thing is when it is at its full, true self. Therefore, glory refers to the manifestation, or the exposure, of the true nature of something.

When the Bible says that the purpose of humanity is to manifest the glory of God, it does not mean just lifting one's hands and saying, "Hallelujah!" That is praise, but it is not glory in the sense in which we are speaking. *Reflecting the glory of God means reflecting His true nature.* God's glory is often best manifested when we respond in a Christlike way in a difficult situation. At that moment, God is saying to you, "Let the glory come out now. Let people see what God is like under pressure."

*Thought*: God's glory is often best manifested when we respond in a Christlike way in a difficult situation.

*Readings*: Isaiah 60:1–3; Philippians 2:14–16

# A WOMAN WHO HONORS GOD

*"Charm is deceptive, and beauty is fleeting; but a woman who fears the* LORD *is to be praised."*          —Proverbs 31:30

Our overview of the purpose and power of women would not be complete without a look at the woman who is considered the epitome of both womanhood and power: the woman of Proverbs 31.

Some women don't even like to read this chapter of the Bible because they are overwhelmed by all the things this woman is apparently able to do! "Well, if I had a staff of servants like she had, I could do all those things, too!" they exclaim. Yet when we consider our exploration of God's purposes for the woman from creation to redemption, and when we think about how the woman has been set free to fulfill His purposes, Proverbs 31 gives us tremendous perspective on what a woman is meant to be. Let us not become overwhelmed when reading about what this woman *does* and miss out on the central message of *who she is.*

One theme that Proverbs 31 communicates is this: The woman is a doer. She is a multitasker (just like many woman today). She is responsible for taking care of her husband, children, home, job, talents, church commitments, charitable work, and sometimes elderly parents. She is a helper *and* she is a leader. She receives seed into her physical, emotional, psychological, and spiritual wombs, incubates it, and then uses it to build and transform the world around her.

Even while a woman is fulfilling all her vital purposes in her home and in the world, she must always remember that *a woman's first place is in God.* Proverbs 31 reminds her, "Don't neglect your relationship with God, and don't forget to develop His character in your inner being as you go about your extremely busy life."

It is much too easy to begin to overlook God when you are taking care of so many other people and responsibilities. Remember, the woman was created to be loved by God and to have fellowship with Him as a spirit-being made in His image. She was meant to reflect His character and likeness, to represent His true nature. God created the woman to have His moral characteristics within her inner being. She is to resemble Him not only as a spirit, but also in these qualities. She was designed to act and function as God does, in love and grace. Therefore, Proverbs 31 is saying, "While you are doing what God has called and gifted you to do, don't forget the importance of His character in your life." That is why it speaks of the *"wife of noble character"* (verse 10).

Having a relationship with the Lord and developing His character in your life form an essential foundation that will strengthen and sustain you in all your activities and accomplishments. With continual refreshing from the Lord, you can purposefully engage in your many responsibilities and fulfill the exciting purposes God has for you.

⟁

*Thought*: It is much too easy to begin to overlook God when you are taking care of so many other people and responsibilities.

*Readings*: Proverbs 31; Colossians 3:1–3

# FREE IN CHRIST

*"It is for freedom that Christ has set us free. Stand firm, then, and do not let yourselves be burdened again by a yoke of slavery."* —Galatians 5:1

Christ has freed the woman and made her an equal partner with the man so that she can fulfill His purposes for her and develop all the gifts that He has given her. He has freed her from the effects of sin and from the oppression that says she is inferior to men.

The world tells us to prove our worth by what we accomplish. The Bible tells us to accept our worth in the One who loves us. You don't have to justify your worth by how much you are doing for others or how many activities you are engaged in. Remember the story of Martha and Mary when Jesus first visited their home? Although Martha was busy preparing a meal for Jesus, He quietly reminded her that Mary had made the better choice by simply sitting at His feet to hear His words of life. (See Luke 10:38–42.)

The woman of Proverbs 31 is not just a busy woman; she is a woman who knows her purpose in God. Let's look at some reasons why this is so:

+ She knows that she is to trust God and draw her strength from Him so that she will not be paralyzed by anxiety; her family and others with whom she is in relationship will be able to put their confidence in her; they will know she has their best interests in mind. (See verses 11–15.)

+ She knows that God values her abilities and intelligence, and so she is free to pursue opportunities and make plans for expanding her realm of influence. (See verses 16–18, 24.)

+ She knows that God is her ultimate Source and that He desires to bless her, so she sets about her work with energy and anticipation. She has a good attitude and doesn't complain. (See verse 17.)

+ Since God has blessed her, she desires to be a blessing to others, and she reaches out to those less fortunate than she. (See verse 20.)

+ Because she knows that her worth comes from her position in God, she treats herself with respect. (See verse 25.)

+ She has immersed herself in God's Word in order to know His ways; therefore, she is able to give godly wisdom and instruction to others. (See verse 26.)

+ Because she has come to know the God of all encouragement, she is an encouragement to her husband, children, friends, and coworkers, and she invests herself in their lives. (See verse 28.)

Sisters in Christ, I wholeheartedly encourage you to pursue all of God's purposes for you. He created your spirit out of His being and out of His love. He designed you perfectly to fulfill your calling in Him. Accept the freedom He has given you in Christ. Know that you are esteemed by Him. Develop the creative ideas He has given you in your innermost being. Use the many gifts and talents He has placed within you. Be the blessing to yourself, your family, and your community that He created you to be.

*Thought*: Accept the freedom God has given you in Christ.

*Readings*: Isaiah 61:1; John 8:36

# ABOUT THE AUTHOR

Dr. Myles Munroe (1954–2014) was an international motivational speaker, best-selling author, educator, leadership mentor, and consultant for government and business. Traveling extensively throughout the world, Dr. Munroe addressed critical issues affecting the full range of human, social, and spiritual development. The central theme of his message is the maximization of individual potential, including the transformation of followers into leaders and leaders into agents of change.

Dr. Munroe was founder and president of Bahamas Faith Ministries International (BFMI), a multidimensional organization headquartered in Nassau, Bahamas. He was chief executive officer and chairman of the board of the International Third World Leaders Association and president of the International Leadership Training Institute.

Dr. Munroe was also the founder and executive producer of a number of radio and television programs aired worldwide. In addition, he was a frequent guest on other television and radio programs and international networks and was a contributing writer for various Bible editions, journals, magazines, and newsletters, such as *The Believer's Topical Bible, The African Cultural Heritage Topical Bible, Charisma Life Christian Magazine,* and *Ministries Today.* He was a popular author of more than forty books, including *The Purpose and Power of the Holy Spirit, The Power of Character in Leadership, The Principles and Power of Vision, Understanding the Purpose and Power of Prayer, Understanding the Purpose and Power of Women, Understanding the Purpose and Power of Men, The Purpose and Power of Authority, The Principles and Benefits of Change, Becoming a Leader,* and *The Spirit of Leadership.* Dr. Munroe has changed the lives of multitudes around the world with a powerful message that inspires, motivates, challenges, and empowers people to discover personal purpose, develop true potential, and manifest their unique leadership abilities. For over thirty years, he trained tens of thousands of leaders in business, industry, education, government, and religion. He personally addressed over 500,000 people each year on personal and professional development. His appeal and message transcend age, race, culture, creed, and economic background.

Dr. Munroe earned B.A. and M.A. degrees from Oral Roberts University and the University of Tulsa, and was awarded a number of honorary doctoral degrees. He also served as an adjunct professor of the Graduate School of Theology at Oral Roberts University.

The parents of two adult children, Charisa and Chairo (Myles Jr.), Dr. Munroe and his wife, Ruth, traveled as a team and were involved in teaching seminars together. Both were leaders who ministered with sensitive hearts and international vision. In November 2014, they were tragically killed in an airplane crash en route to an annual leadership conference sponsored by Bahamas Faith Ministries International. A statement from Dr. Munroe in his book *The Power of Character in Leadership* summarizes his own legacy: "Remember that character ensures the longevity of leadership, and men and women of principle will leave important legacies and be remembered by future generations."

# Welcome to Our House!

## *We Have a Special Gift for You*

It is our privilege and pleasure to share in your love of Christian books. We are committed to bringing you authors and books that feed, challenge, and enrich your faith.

To show our appreciation, we invite you to sign up to receive a specially selected **Reader Appreciation Gift**, with our compliments. Just go to the Web address at the bottom of this page.

God bless you as you seek a deeper walk with Him!

WE HAVE A GIFT FOR YOU. VISIT:

whpub.me/nonfictionthx

WHITAKER
HOUSE